Advanced Pra___ ___

"I am obsessed. Obsessed with this book and the power it provides moms who are in the midst of chaos to focus on planning for their very own best lives. This book should be given to each new mom as they leave the hospital with their new baby (to implement after the sleep deprivation wears off). *How To Design Your Life* isn't a book that hypes you to quit your job and find a new hustle - it's a bible on how to get clear on what your passions are, how to stay consistent to achieve your goals, and how to maximize and invest your time and get creative to give time back into yourself."

- Carrie G, mom of three, wife, practicing attorney,
and founder of @carriesbookclub

"This book is an intimate conversation with your most supportive girlfriend — the one who just 'gets it'. She holds your hand and cheers you on every step of the way while simultaneously keeping it all very real. *How to Design Your Life* has methodically empowered me to do a little better today than yesterday. Read it twice: once to learn it, another to live it. An absolute must read!"

- Dawn B, working mom of two

"Sharon gets it. From the moment I read the first page, it was clear. I am a busy mom of two very busy boys and found this to be an easy refreshing read that sparked motivation almost instantly. Sharon has done the hard work for us by condensing all of the great takeaways from countless self-help books into one seamless blueprint that can be used at any stage of your journey. I feel confident that my future and the future of my family is headed for success by applying these habits into our everyday lives. Post it notes and MAP books will be keeping us accountable!"

- Danielle H, working mom of two active boys

"If you've been looking for the book to help you take your vision and make it a plan that you can stick with, this is the book. This has actionable steps and breaks down how to create a plan in a way that is not overwhelming. In fact it breaks it down in a way that makes you excited to start working toward your vision. This book is concise yet it feels like she is talking right to you. Sharon makes it feel like you are sitting down with her having a morning tea and talking about everything in life. The good, the bad, the tough conversation, the conversations that bring you joy, and the dreams that excite you but you are too scared to say out loud."

- Jessica, small business mom of one boy

"This book is pure joy. Written by a busy mom, for busy moms, it is helpful and insightful without adding more pressure or stress into our already busy lives. Sharon takes us on her personal journey, as she gives tips and tricks she has learned along the way. She shares her own trials, errors, and successes as a busy mom, which are incredibly relatable. By the end of the book, you feel like you have a new friend / cheerleader in your corner - and who doesn't need that?! The ideas provided in this book can be started right away, but with lots of grace and patience to take baby steps so as to not get too overwhelmed. You can pick and choose what works for you depending on the "season" you are in at the moment. The stories and humor through-out the book make it an easy and enjoyable read. If you are a busy mom that needs practical ideas to help you get control of your busy and crazy life right away - then this is the book you need!"

- Stephanie C, working mom of two boys

How To Design Your Life

SHARON LEGER

HOW TO
design
YOUR
LIFE

A Busy Mom's Roadmap
to Creating a Life You
Are **Obsessed** With

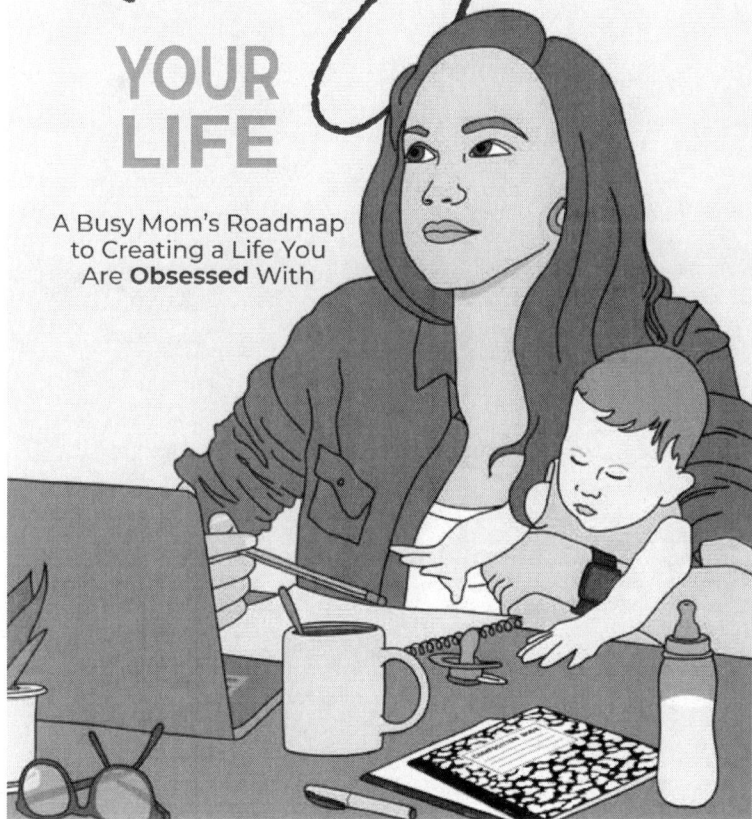

Hardcover: ISBN 979-8-218-34625-6
Paperback: 979-8-218-33231-0
Ebook: 979-8-218-34624-9

First Edition: January 2024

Cover Art by Laura Murray Creative
Interior Layout by Laura Murray Creative

Download your
free resources!

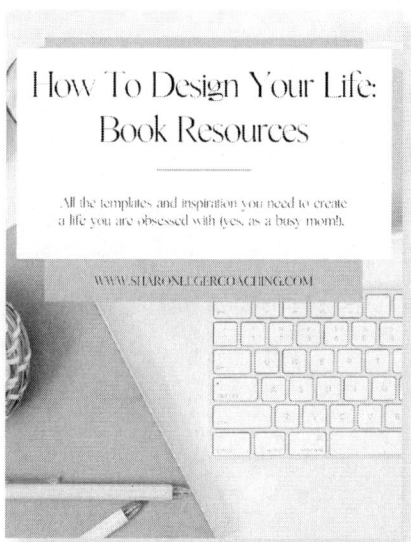

How To Design Your Life:
Book Resources

All the templates and inspiration you need to create
a life you are obsessed with (yes, as a busy mom).

WWW.SHARONLEGERCOACHING.COM

As a busy mom, you have a lot going on.

That is why I put all the downloads you'll need to make
the most out of this book, all in one place.

You can check it out on my website at
www.sharonlegercoaching.com/how-to-design-your-life

To Aubrey and Alyssa, it was always for you.

TABLE OF CONTENTS

1   **Introduction: Your Time Is Now**
2   From Overwhelmed To Empowered
6   How This Book Is Going To Change Your Life
8   Why This Book? Why Now?
10   How To Make The Most Of Your Investment
11   Let's Make A Plan!

Section One: Preparing The Foundation For Your Dream Life

17   **Chapter One: What's Personal Growth Got To Do With It?**
18   It All Begins With This
19   But Seriously, What Is Personal Growth?
20   Personal Growth For Busy Moms
22   Thinking About What Personal Growth Isn't
23   The Personal Growth Triangle
26   Let's Make A Plan!

27   **Chapter Two: Get Organized**
28   Why You Need An Organizational System
29   What Is A Map Book, Anyway?
29   How A Notebook System Will Accelerate Your Growth
31   Utilizing Your Map Book Weekly & Daily
33   Maximizing Your Map Book's Potential
33   Monthly Pages
33   Future Lists
34   Random Lists
35   Let's Make A Plan!

37   **Chapter Three: Assessing Your Current Context**
38   Using A Reflection Wheel To Figure Out Where You Are
46   Identifying Your Level 10 Life
47   Achieving Your Level 10 Life
47   Gaining Traction On Your Level 10 Life
48   Curating Your Dream Life

49   Designing Your Dream Life Vision
51   Let's Make A Plan!

Section Two: Designing Your Dream Life

55 Chapter Four: Creating Your Dream Life Vision
56   Stratgy 1: Dream Life Vision Exercise
57   Mind Map
58   Strategy 2: Ideal Day Exercise
59   Strategy 3: Creating A (Dream Life) Vision Board
61   Making Your Dream Life Your Real Life
61   Step 1: Identify What You Want
62   Step 2: Explore The Potential Steps To Get There
65   Step 3: Strategize And Systemize
66   Step 4: Take Consistent Action
67   Final Words About Consistent Action
67   Step 5: Align/Course-Correct

71 Chapter Five: Time Maximization For Busy Moms
72   Getting Clear On Your Time
72   Time Tracker
72   Identifying What You Need
75   Things I Need Every Day/Week/Month/Year Exercise
76   Reimagine Your Time
78   An Ideal Day Example
80   Getting Clear On What Matters In This Season
81   How To Plan When You're Overwhelmed
83   Becoming More Present With Your Loved Ones
83   Step 1: Set Clear Expectations
84   Step 2: Manage Technology
84   Step 3: Do A Thought Download
84   Step 4: Set Aside Time On Your Calendar
85   Step 5: Be Honest With Yourself And Your Child
86   Let's Make A Plan!

87 Chapter Six: Living In Alignment With Your Core Values
88   Defining Core Values
88   Why Core Values Matter
89   Strategically Living In Alignment With Your Core Values
90   Step 1: Complete A Values Assessment
91   Step 2: Create A Mission Statement
94   Step 3: Revisit Your Dream Life Vision

95   Step 4: Consider Who You Want To Be
97   Let's Make A Plan!

Section Three: Start Living A Life You Are Obsessed With Today

101   **Chapter Seven: Goal-Setting For Busy Moms**
102   Getting It All Out Of Your Head: Brain Dump/Mind Sweep
107   Strategizing This Quarter: Quarterly Check-Ins
109   Getting Consistent: Weekly Check-Ins
109   Purposefully Bringing It All Together: How To Plan Your Year
110   Step 1: How To Plan Your Year
111   Step 2: Vision Of My Life In 365 Days
112   Step 3: Create Your Yearly Goals
113   Step 4: Create Family Goals
114   Step 5: Create Personal Goals
114   Kicking It Up A Notch: Going From 12-Month To 12-Week Goals
118   Setting Goals When You Are Overwhelmed
118   Let's Make A Plan!

121   **Chapter Eight: Establishing Positive Daily Habits**
122   Identifying Positive Habits
125   Accountability: Tracking Your Habits
125   Visually Track Your Streaks
126   Habit Tracker
127   Tracking Habits In Your Map Book
128   There's An App For That
129   Accountability Group
130   Implementing High-Leverage Systems
132   Creating Your Own Systems
133   My Morning System
134   Staying Accountable
135   How Systems Will Change Your Life
136   Decide Once
136   Remove The Emotion
136   The Compound Effect
137   Consistency > Intensity
        Let's Make A Plan!

139   **Chapter Nine: Finding Your Passions**
140   Finding My Passions: The Happiness Project
141   Identifying Your Passions
143   Wander A Library Or Bookstore

144   Search Job Listings
145   Check Out College Course Catalogs
146   Create A Life Experiences List
147   Some Common Mom Struggles
147   Struggle #1: I Don't Have Time
148   Struggle #2: There Isn't Anything I'm Passionate About I Haven't Already Pursued
149   Struggle #3: My Kids' Activities Consume So Much Time There's No Time For My Activities
151   Let's Make A Plan!

153   **Chapter Ten: Creating Your Dream Life Action Plan**
154   Creating Your Three-Year Action Plan
155   Why 3 Years?
155   Designing Your Roadmap To Your Dream Life
155   Step 1: Brainstorm What You Want Your Life To Look Like In Three Years
156   Step 2: Refine
158   Step 3: Create Distinct Action Steps
162   Common Struggles
162   Struggle #1: This Feels Overwhelming
163   Struggle #2: I Don't Have Time
164   Struggle #3: I Don't Even Know What I Want My Dream Life To Look Like
165   Struggle #4: I Don't Have Enough Ideas
166   Struggle #5: I Have Too Many Ideas!
168   Struggle #6: Nothing Can Change (Aka Fixed Mindset)
169   Embarking On Your Dream Life
172   Upgrade Your Life Today
174   Let's Make A Plan!

175   **Conclusion: Your Dream Life Awaits**
187   A Final Word

189   Acknowledgments
191   Index
195   About The Author

INTRODUCTION

Your Time
Is Now!

Five years ago, I was sitting in my Nissan Pathfinder, waiting to turn left at the light to go to my school where I was a fifth-grade teacher. With my blinker clicking methodically, a debilitating thought struck me: I was thirty-two years old and had thirty-two years left to go to a job I hated.

Essentially, my entire lifetime. That thought gutted me. I knew in my heart that I just couldn't do it. To be honest, I was not sure how I was going to make it through the day. Nevertheless, the next thirty-two years! I knew I would never want my daughters to go to a job every day that left them feeling unfulfilled and hopeless. But what the heck was I going to do about it? This was my life, and I felt stuck in it.

To be honest, at the time, I really did not know what I was going to do. I had no backup plan, no safety net to fall back into. I had landed what I thought was my dream life, the life I had once dreamed about as an eighteen-year-old college student. I had gotten the "dream job," married an

1

amazing man, bought a home, and had two beautiful daughters. So why wasn't I happy? How was it possible that I was no longer feeling fulfilled in the dream life I had outgrown?

I know I'm not alone in this story. But I also know that there are thousands of moms in similar situations who don't feel like they can change their circumstances. And trust me, I get it. But what would happen if you used that pit in your stomach as a catalyst to design your dream life instead of as an excuse?

Spoiler alert: do you know what saved me? Personal growth—and a whole lot of it. When I hit my lowest low at the traffic light that day, I knew that something had to change. The part that terrified me the most? I was pretty sure that the thing that needed to change was me. Looking back, I am so grateful for that moment, and I still give a little smile as I sail through that intersection now, looking forward to my future instead of feeling trapped by it.

My personal growth journey led me to some pretty unexpected places. Even now, as I write this, I am in disbelief that I was able to create this dream life that I am in love with in just the span of a few short years. Not to mention, all of this happened while working full-time and being a full-time mom and wife. If I can do it, you can do it too, Mama.

From Overwhelmed to Empowered

Similarly to a lot of my coaching clients, I was raised with a super strong sense of loyalty and a deep desire for stability. I believed at my core that I always had to finish what I started, no matter how I felt about it or how happy I was. So, when I got my teaching degree and landed my dream teaching job—boom! Instant plan for the next thirty-seven and a half years of my life. With that teaching job, I could literally tell you what I'd be doing fifteen years to the day. At the time, that made me absolutely giddy. Stability? Check. Loyalty? Double check.

The first two years of teaching were good. My husband and I got married, everything seemed to be working out according to "plan." However, in the seven years that followed, the wheels started to fall off the bus. I quickly realized that I was stuck in a life that wasn't my dream life. And to be honest, it wasn't even close.

In my third year of teaching, I was physically attacked by a parent at a parent-teacher conference. That experience rattled me to my core and caused my anxiety to skyrocket. I finally realized I needed help when I refused to get out of the car one date night because I was afraid we would bump into the mom who attacked me. I began therapy shortly after that. And while therapy helped, being in the classroom where I had no administrative support was a challenge every single day. I no longer felt safe at work, and the constant berating from parents ruined me. To this day, I can honestly say that I still love the students, and my passion for teaching is still going strong. But something changed in me that third year in the classroom.

From there on out, I put a smile on my face every day and kept showing up until late 2014, when my first daughter was born. My husband and I worked really hard to save up for an extended maternity leave. Because of that, I was able to take a leave of absence from teaching to be home with her for almost ten months.

During that time away from the classroom, I desperately looked for a way out of teaching. Most of my efforts were put into actively helping my husband look for higher-paying administrative positions. I figured if he could get a school administrator job, we would make up for my paycheck, and I would not have to go back to work. I had a feeling that being a stay-at-home mom was not going to be for me, but I was willing to try if it meant I could leave the classroom.

My husband got heartbreakingly close to locking in an administrative position half a dozen times, but in the end, none of them worked out. I was devastated. A few months before I was set to go back to work, I applied for a few jobs myself but rejected the interviews when they called. Nothing felt right, and I was terrified about our financial situation if I made any big changes. We also knew that we wanted to have another child, and I did not want to give up another potentially long (unpaid) maternity leave by starting a new job. So, by the time August rolled around, I resigned myself to the fact that I was stuck and returned to the classroom.

Around that same time, I slowly began to start exploring the idea of personal growth. This is embarrassing to even admit, but I was so mortified by the stigma of personal growth and self-help that it took me a few weeks to muster the courage to even take a personal growth book out of the library (it was Stephen Covey's *The Seven Habits of Highly Effective People*, in case you're curious). Progress was slow, but I was grateful that I was at least doing something to grow into the role model that I wanted to be for my daughter.

That is also about the time that I discovered Rachel Hollis. Although she has recently fallen from grace, her book, *Girl Wash Your Face*, helped me to discover that it's okay to want more for your life. She taught me that you don't have to settle for a life that you're not genuinely excited about. So, while it wasn't a huge AH-HA moment, the seed had been planted.

Fast-forward to January of 2018, the winter after my final maternity leave with my second daughter. This was the day of the Traffic Light Revelation, and I parked my car at school with a new question ringing in my head: this was my situation...what the heck was I going to do about it?

What was the NEW plan?! At the time, it was the dead of winter, and my seasonal affective depressive disorder was hitting hard. I was working full-time and felt myself sliding deeper down every day. I wasn't the mom

I wanted to be for my kids or the partner I wanted to be for my husband. One desperate afternoon, I made a list of things that I was interested in. I just wanted something to excite me again. To be honest, I wanted to prove to myself that I could still GET excited about something. There were a bunch of half-hearted things on the list, and I just picked the one that intrigued me the most: photography. While I battled my rut, I figured I would learn to use my expensive camera that my dad had bought us as a wedding present. I found a free online course through Pinterest and immediately got hooked.

My husband was so excited to see me start to pull myself out of my winter rut that he didn't think twice when I asked him if we could take $500 from our savings to put toward an online photography class. This left our savings account at a dangerously low level, but at that point, it was desperate times, and we did not even care.

I had literally NO time to do the class (remember, I was teaching full-time, and we had two kids under the age four). So, I decided that I had to create my own time. I began devouring books and podcasts about how to maximize your time and discovered amazing authors like Darren Hardy and Mel Robbins. They inspired me to take advantage of my situation, and I started waking up at 4:00 AM to go through the content of my online photography class. It was too dark to practice in the morning, so I'd run home after school to apply what I learned before the sun would set at 5:00 PM (yay, New England).

I swore up and down that I'd never turn my photography hobby into a business, but then, on August 1st, I launched "Sharon Leger Photography" with all of the confidence that I had gained in my year-long personal growth journey. The rest, they say, is history.

When a part-time literacy interventionist position came up at my school that May, I used my newfound confidence and growth mindset to take the leap and apply. My husband and I celebrated the day that I got the job, and I knew that I was slowly making my Traffic Light Revelation a thing of the past. My new job had me working three days a week, so I was able to dedicate one full day a week to my business and one full day to my girls, a time that I knew I would never regret. Once COVID hit, I took an extended absence and then finally resigned from my teaching job in May of 2021. I can honestly say I haven't looked back.

Friends, all that was three years ago. Since then, I realized how much I needed a dream life vision to make huge changes in my life. Now, I am sitting in my own photography studio as a full-time family photographer and helping to empower other busy moms to be the best version of themselves. I have a protocol that I now rely on to hold myself to high standards, especially during the longer winter months. I am excited to go to work every day, and I go to sleep at night knowing that I am modeling for my girls how to live their lives on purpose, even if it's not always easy. I have a dream life that I am actively moving toward each and every day by following my action plan. And I want you to join me, Mama.

How This Book Will Change Your Life

The intention behind this book is NOT for you to start your own business, quit your job, write a book, start a podcast, or do what I did. My intention is for you to feel like you have direction, support, and the ability to create a PLAN to live a life you are obsessed with. Everyone's journey is going to look different, and that is more than okay. It's just about growing into the best version of yourself, both for you and for your family. And who doesn't want that?!

So if you decide to follow along on this journey, you are going to learn:
- What personal growth is and how it will accelerate your progress toward your dream life.
- How to go from overwhelmed to proactive with a cus-

tomized organizational system.

- A consistent way to assess your current context and determine your best next steps.
- How to find your passions as a busy mom.
- Time maximization techniques to make the most of the time you do have.
- How to establish your top five core values and use those to structure your growth journey.
- Inspiration about habits, routines, and systems that will have you feeling like you are on the fast track to your dream life vision.
- And finally, how to create an action plan that will help you know what steps you need to take over the next three years to bring your dream life vision to reality.

When I first started on my own dream life journey, I scoured the Internet for resources for moms. There had to be someone out there who got it. Someone who understood having to get to daycare pick-up on time, having to RSVP to all the birthday parties, and who wanted more for themselves and their families. And, Mama, I struggled to find that. There just wasn't anything out there.

Every time I picked up a book at Barnes and Noble and looked at the back, the old guy with grown kids smiled back at me, promising me he was going to help me manage my time better. Doubtful, Dude-That-Never-Has-To-Pack-A-Nut-Free-Lunch. I wanted a fellow mom who got it, who could just tell me what to do as I stood in the middle of the bookstore, wondering if I had outlived my last dry shampoo treatment.

Without a mentor to help me, I realized that I would have to design the dream life I sought on my own. So I figured it out. I researched, read every personal growth book I could get my hands on, and experimented. I wrote, created, and designed a life that I was excited to wake up for in the morning. Occasionally, I cried. But by the end, I look back on my journey and feel nothing but gratitude for the struggles and perspective I gained along the way.

And now, I want to share that dream life roadmap with you.

Why This Book? Why Now?

Five years ago, the personal growth section at Barnes and Noble was Five years ago, the personal growth section at Barnes and Noble was maybe three shelves. Now, rows upon rows of books are dedicated to self-improvement and personal development. While this is beyond amazing, it is also humbling to realize that most of them are not for us—the moms in the trenches who want to make a big change while the clock of our children's childhoods is ticking loudly in our ears.

This book is for you if:
- You know in your gut that you are ready for a change ... you just have no idea where to start.
- You feel yourself wanting someone to just tell you what to do.
- You created your dream life but are now stuck, feeling like you wanted more and feeling mom guilt for thinking that way.
- You have always been intrigued by others who have changed their lives, but feel like you could never be brave/strong/courageous (insert your own adjective here) enough to do it.
- You are ready to start living a life you are genuinely excited about.

And why now? It's time. It's time for you to create a life that your children want to emulate. It's time to pull yourself up by your bootstraps and get the support and motivation you need to make a real change. After all, little eyes are always watching.

Stick with me for a minute. I am a sucker for a good metaphor (it's the English major in me): the best parallel I can share with you is that I strongly believe that your kids should see you work out. What does this have to do with personal growth? I believe kids should see you work out, see the messy process, instead of just seeing the end result. If you only work out when your kids are at daycare, sleeping, or at Grandma's house, they will never see the literal sweat that goes into that progress.

> "Waiting until your kids no longer 'need' you is not a good enough reason to not change your reality today."

It is the same for your personal growth. Waiting until your kids no longer "need" you is not a good enough reason to not change your reality today. If you are not happy right now, your kids feel that. They see the frustration, the stress, and the anxiety. And not only do they see it, but they feel it too. Your job as their parent is to acknowledge what is not working and start putting in the work. One day, they may find themselves in a similar situation. And don't you want them to look back on their childhood, remember what you did, and follow suit? That is what I thought!

When I went back to work after my first maternity leave, a loving colleague reassured me with, "You are showing your daughter what it means to be a working mom since she will be doing the same thing some day." At first, I remember that thought being extremely comforting. But as I got more and more dissatisfied with my current life context, I began to realize that my daughter had a front-row seat to my miserable experience in a career

I no longer loved. It was time to flip the script. I wanted her to see me recreating my dream life, with time for her to enjoy the happy mom that was going to come from the process.

How To Make The Most Of This Investment

Personal growth is the best investment that you can make in yourself. Now, don't get me wrong. I am not necessarily talking about a financial investment here, despite the fact that I will say I have invested thousands of dollars into my personal growth journey over time. But at the beginning, your personal growth investment is mainly going to be your time. When you pick up this book and commit to it, you are agreeing that, yes, you are going to make yourself a priority, and you are going to do it now.

As an avid book lover, I can admit that I have several books that I have purchased with gusto, then allowed to sit, dusty and unread on my shelf. Mama, make yourself a promise right now. Not this book, not this time.

This time, you are making an investment. Again, not just a financial investment but an emotional investment in yourself. By picking up this book, you are acknowledging that you are ready to live a life you are obsessed with. Today is Day One. It is time to stop telling yourself the story that "one day" you will tackle your personal growth. One day, when you're less tired, have more job security, are with a better partner. Let that story go. You are no longer waiting. You are showing up for your life right now, today, on center stage with your kids in the front row.

The time that you invest in yourself now is going to pay off—both now and in the future. When you take an hour to read through a chapter and your daughter sees you taking notes in your notebook, a little light bulb is going to go off in her mind. If you swing by the library and take out two books on personal growth, your son will more than likely notice. By modeling this new lifestyle, this openness to growth, you are going to start a domino effect that you will reap the rewards of for years to come, I promise.

Let's Make A Plan!

Throughout this book, each chapter concludes with a concrete action step or two that you can take action on right away. These action steps are going to take you thirty minutes or less to accomplish and will help to jumpstart your progress with the content shared in the chapter.

At the conclusion of this book, there is a concrete summary and action plan for you to follow. So whether you want to read the whole book straight through or take it one chapter at a time, you have a resource to guide you.

Finally, many of the free resources listed in this book are shared on my website– www.sharonlegercoaching.com. From there, you can download templates, examples, etc., to help guide you on your journey.

LET'S MAKE A PLAN!

- Create a timeline of your life up until this point in your MAP Book (significant events, years, etc.):
- In the left-hand column, write the current year.
- In the middle column, any major life events that happened that year (started a job, had a baby, got married, etc.).
- In the right-hand column, write down any important takeaways from that year or season of life.

year	Life Event	What I Learned
2005	Graduate from college	• Needed to make some lifestyle changes after college • Budgeting is not optional
2014	Had 1st baby	• Boundaries for work - can't be bringing things home & working all weekend
2016	Had 2nd baby	• The most important thing is for my kids to have a happy mom.

You can start from the year you were born or start after high school. Whatever makes the most sense for you! If you are over the top, like me, you can even break this down by month. Obviously, not every month is going to have anything significant in it, but it will help you later as you begin to track your dream life journey.

There is something so rewarding about seeing everything that you have accomplished in your life in one space. Take a moment to acknowledge all of your efforts, Mama. Indulge yourself for a minute and think about where your life might be at this time next year if you commit to your dream life journey and begin to create a life you are excited to wake up for every day.

Up Next

In Chapter One, you will:
- Learn why you need personal growth in order to create and live a life you love.
- Discover how you can accelerate your progress toward your dream life vision through personal growth.
- Begin to develop your growth mindset.

Preparing
The Foundation
For Your Dream Life

CHAPTER ONE

What's Personal Growth Got To Do With It?

Before you can even start to think about designing your dream life, you first need to tackle the idea of personal growth. When I first sit down with many of my coaching clients, they often start off by admitting to me that "personal growth" feels like a dirty word. Self-help or personal development almost sounds like something that you do not want to talk about within earshot of your kids. This makes complete sense to me. Like other processes we do not want to talk about in front of our kids, personal growth is intimate. It is personal, it is vulnerable, and for a lot of people, it can be wrapped up in their self-worth and bring their confidence into question.

And talking about personal growth with your peers? No, thank you! What if they think you're miserable? What if they stage an intervention? What if they think you're not grateful for the life you have?

If you have ever felt that way about personal growth, you are not alone. And by personal growth, of course, I also mean self-help, personal development, self-improvement, and whatever other lingo that has been used to describe the concept of improving yourself to reach your highest potential.

As a former English major, I choose my words carefully, and personal growth is the term that I most often use to describe this journey. To me, the idea of growth is so important because you are not simply "improving" or "developing." You are evolving, growing, and changing as you apply what you are learning.

By the end of this chapter, you will have a true understanding of what personal growth is and its role in helping you to make your dream life your real life.

It All Begins With This

My personal growth journey began in the first chapter of John Maxwell's book, 15 Invaluable Laws of Growth. I had always been interested in the idea of learning more about yourself and working to improve areas of your life that you felt were lacking, but that's as far as I had ever gotten. To be honest, before I picked up Maxwell's book, it actually didn't even occur to me to have a plan for my personal growth. And that's really saying something because I have a plan for EVERYTHING!

In the book, Maxwell asked: "What is your plan for personal growth?" That hit me—hard. It literally took my breath away. Because for all the plans that I had as a mom—a maternity leave plan, a dinner plan, a when we're going to get a new roof on the house plan—it didn't ever occur to me that I needed a plan for myself and my growth. How could I not have a plan for that?!

From that moment on, I promised myself that my personal growth wouldn't be an accident. I would take the wheel of my personal growth journey and make things happen. Didn't like my job? Changed it. Frustrated with the lack of communication in my marriage? Fixed it. No time to learn photography? Made it.

Whenever I am asked to define personal growth, this quote from Ed Mylett always pops into my mind: "My dream is that at the end of my life when I meet the man I could have become, the best version of myself... we are identical twins. For me, that is heaven." Who is that ideal version of me? What else could my life look like? I challenge myself every day to move closer to those ideals. For me, that is personal growth.

But Seriously, What Is Personal Growth?

Before we can really get into what personal growth looks like for busy moms specifically, we need to define what personal growth is.

After reading hundreds, if not thousands, of personal growth books over the years, I have culminated all of the definitions that I have come across into this one: personal growth is a learning journey that you purposefully embark on to bring you closer to the best version of yourself.

No matter what your definition is of personal growth, I think we can all agree that personal growth is about trying new things and being inspired. It's about finding your passions and leaning into them. Most importantly, it's about modeling for your kids how someone can strategically create positive change that can propel them toward their dream life.

When you are on a personal growth journey, the person you are going to be in a year, three years, or five years is beyond your imagination right now. Definitely not in a bad way, but growth is inevitable. You will find yourself achieving successes you never thought possible, hitting milestones faster than you ever dreamed you could, and crushing your goals, all while still making it in time to grab a spot in the carpool lane.

Personal growth is about creating the dream life that you are excited to wake up for every morning. Can you confidently say that you are excited to hop out of bed every morning to live another day in your life? If the answer is heck no, then I am so excited for you. What you are about to dream, strategize, and implement is going to fundamentally change you. One day, in the not-too-distant future, you will look back on this moment and point to it, saying, "That. That was the moment I decided that I was going to change my life. And I did."

Personal Growth For Busy Moms

Okay, okay. So you are all hyped up now to get started on your personal growth journey and start living your dream life. Maybe you still have a nagging voice in the back of your head, wondering how you are going to make time for this. Or how you are going to sell it to your partner (spoiler alert: you do not have to). Maybe you are struggling to quiet that voice that says, "This book is not for you. It is for all the brave moms." Hard stop. Stop it right now. This book is for you. It is in your hands right now for a reason, and despite your schedule, the ages of your children, or how tired you feel after a long day, you can do this. It is going to look a little different than what personal development gurus are preaching, though, because, as a mom, so much depends on you. But guess what? That is not going to be our excuse. That is going to be our superpower.

This all leads us to the question: what does personal growth look like for busy moms? And how does that growth look different than it does for other populations?

I recently had a friend tell me that if she picks up a book or reads a blog post about a personal growth topic, she'll immediately check to see if the person is a parent. If they aren't, she immediately drops the book or closes the tab and moves on to other things. That person "just doesn't get it," in her words. Tell me that doesn't resonate with you, Mama. We don't want to waste the precious time we have to better ourselves, immersing ourselves in ideas that will just lead to more frustration, overwhelm, and burnout. We don't have time for that!

As a busy mom, your personal growth is just that—it's personal. But it's also about your family, your role in your family, and how you are able to show up for them every single day.

Personal growth for busy moms looks different because little eyes are watching. That is both a blessing and a curse. I am a firm believer that our kids should see our messy middle. They should see the bickering with your husband over whose turn it is to take out the trash, they should see you working out to strengthen your body, and they should see you cry when you're sad. Sheltering our kiddos from these realities seems cruel in a way, to later send them out into the world where they will have to navigate these struggles without a model to refer back to. Personal growth is the same way.

> "When we believe that we can take on the impossible, they begin to think that maybe they can, too. And isn't that what we want for them? Isn't that the ultimate mom goal?"

A few nights ago, my husband was reading to my oldest daughter before bed. The character in the book mentioned wanting to start a business. Another character assured him that that was an impossible task. My daughter immediately told my husband: "It's not impossible. Mommy did it!" I'm pretty sure my heart grew two sizes when my husband repeated the conversation to me later. Our kids are watching. We need to be the example that we want them to follow. When we believe that we can take on the impossible, they begin to think that maybe they can, too. And isn't that what we want for them? Isn't that the ultimate mom goal?

The final way that personal growth looks different for busy moms is because our priorities are different than a counterpart with fewer responsibilities. As moms, we think about our time differently: we don't have hours to spend reading lengthy books that don't further our journeys or free weekends to go to conferences. Any time invested in ourselves needs to be meaningful. And ideally, the time invested will be returned to our family in the form of a better version of ourselves.

So, as you start to think about what personal growth means to you, keep in mind that you will need to give yourself grace. You will need to make hard decisions and have challenging conversations. Personal growth is not easy, but it definitely will be worth it if you take the time to decide how it is going to show up in your life each and every day.

Thinking About What Personal Growth Isn't

I spent ten years teaching fifth grade. Whenever we dug deep into a definition, I always took the time to explore the opposite of the word. So now that we have an idea of what personal growth IS, what is it NOT?

First, being on a personal growth journey does not mean you are broken. It doesn't mean you're miserable at your job, that you're not present with your kids, or that you're in an unhappy relationship. It just means that you want to lean into all of these areas in order to show up as the best version of yourself. If there was one personal growth myth that I could dispel with a wave of my hand, this would be the one.

Second, personal growth is not a diet plan or a workout regimen. Actually, personal growth rarely has anything to do with your personal appearance at all. So many moms confuse their personal wellness journey with personal growth. While there are many overlaps, and fitness can be a great way to apply a lot of personal growth principles, they are different.

Next, if I could shout this from the rooftops, I would: personal growth is NOT time management. I'm going to say it again for the moms in the back: personal growth is NOT time management. You are BUSY, Mama. You don't need more time to squeeze in more things. You do enough. You are enough. Are we going to talk about time management? We are, but only in the context of time maximization and prioritization, putting the first things first.

And finally, personal growth is not a one-size-fits-all path. Personal growth is customized for each person, and it looks different for everyone. The information that you gather from this book is going to help you to create your own path, identify your own goals for your journey. Just because two moms want to reach similar goals or dream lives does not mean they are going to take the same steps to get there. Your timeline is likely going to be very different from others. Maybe you will be faster, maybe you will be slower. So many factors play into this, like your comfort level with your growth, your confidence, and your mindset. With all that being said, be patient with yourself and trust that things will work out the way that they should.

Personal Growth Triangle

When I first began to create content for busy moms and meet with coaching clients to plan their growth journeys, I quickly came upon a major realization. Looking back, it seems quite obvious, but at the time it was a light bulb moment for me: not all moms are at the same place in their journeys. Some moms come to me and tell me that they have never once thought about their personal growth explicitly. Yet, as we dive in, I realize that they have advanced systems and routines in place and are consistently working towards their life goals. Sure, they never called it "personal growth", but that is exactly what it was.

On the flip side, I would have moms who promised me they were years into their personal growth journeys. Upon some further digging, I would uncover that they did not have an organizational system, basic routines or control over some of the essentials, such as sleep, nutrition, finances, or exercise. There is absolutely no shame with where you are on your personal growth journey. But knowing where you are is going to guide you to the next steps that will help you to grow more effectively and efficiently. If I am trying to inspire a new client with an advanced strategy when they do not have the basics down, I am setting them up for failure. That mom, who is not yet ready for an advanced system, will get overwhelmed and frustrated, right off the bat.

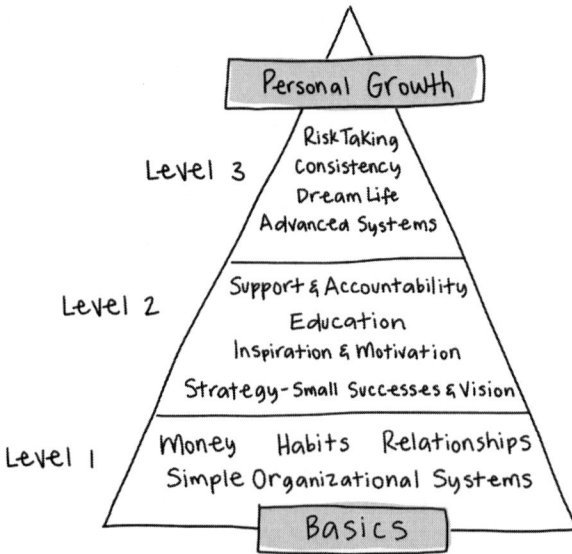

That is why I created the personal growth triangle. Like Maslow's hierarchy of needs, this triangle rests on a firm base of foundational skills that are essential for personal growth (Level One). The base of the triangle can not be overlooked and if you find yourself struggling to get consistent on your personal growth journey, I would highly recommend that you pause and reconsider how confident you feel in Level One of your personal growth triangle.

What is Level One of the personal growth triangle? As previously mentioned, Level One is the essential habits and systems that are required for growth. Moms that are in Level One are working to get consistent with daily habits, basic budgeting, nutrition, and general time maximization. Once those foundational skills are developed, then these moms are ready for Level Two work on the personal growth triangle. The majority of moms that I meet begin here, at Level One and if this is you, you are not alone!

The second level of the triangle is more complex. This is where my clients are ready for education, inspiration, accountability, and support. They are creating more intense systems and are getting super consistent with their habits. To be honest, this is probably the most exciting level of growth. So many moms actually spend years here and it really is not a bad place to be. There are so many ideas and inspirational people to discover at this level and so much growth can be made on Level Two alone.

Finally, the third level of the triangle is where I consider myself today. This is where the basics have been established, tons of education and inspiration have occurred and someone is ready or is actively making major changes to their lives in order to align with their new growth values.

Now that you have an understanding of the three levels of personal growth, ask yourself: where am I on the personal growth triangle today? By taking the time to strengthen your skills at each level, you will be setting yourself up to accelerate on your personal growth journey, to create a life you are obsessed with in a sustainable, scalable way.

LET'S MAKE A PLAN!

Take some time to consider what personal growth means to you at this stage in your life. You can journal about it or just think about what activities you associate with the idea of personal growth. There may be some mindset shifts to be made here, so be honest with yourself!

Up Next

In Chapter Two, you will:

- Figure out if you are in need of an organizational system (spoiler alert: you probably are).
- Create your custom organizational system in sixty minutes or less so you can start making progress toward your dream life today!

CHAPTER TWO

Get Organized!

Megan was a new client, and she had been on my calendar for a few weeks now. The day of our meeting, I was so surprised when twenty minutes went by and no Megan! I double-checked the reminder email, and yup, she had opened it. When I called her, it went straight to voicemail. After sending over a text, I quickly received a reply: "Oh my goodness, I totally forgot that was today! I am SO sorry!"

Needless to say, when we did have our first meeting, the first challenge Megan wanted to focus on was getting herself organized. As a single mom with three boys, she constantly felt like her head was going to explode. Megan admitted that she had trouble sleeping at night because she would lay there, trying to remember everything she had forgotten to do.

If this sounds familiar, you are in the right place. This chapter is not going to recommend that you fold your shirts a certain way or do laundry on Thursdays. You are going to learn how to create an organizational system that helps you get everything out of your brain and consistently use this system to reduce overwhelm, anxiety, and stress. Once this is done, you will have the capacity to pursue your dream life, knowing nothing is going to fall through the cracks. And how amazing would that feel?!

Why You Need An Organizational System

Let me guess: before you had kids, you were more or less able to get by with daily to-do lists on sticky notes and a Google calendar? Maybe a new planner from Target once in a while? And one day, maybe one day recently, you realized that your life was getting too complex for a 3x3 sticky note? If this is you, you need a system, Mama!

Here are a few signs that a notebook organizational system might be for you:

- In the last week, you have spent more than five minutes hunting for that orange sticky note on which you wrote an important phone number (we've all done it: "I know it's orange, I know it's here...somewhere!").
- You have snapped at someone you love just because you were overwhelmed, stressed, and felt like you were the only one steering the ship.
- Like Megan, you lay in bed at night and think of everything that you forgot to get done.
- You notice that you are beginning to miss deadlines, feel constantly on the verge of a panic attack, and just don't know where to start.

If this sounds like you, it may be time to give this notebook organizational system a try. If you are ready to start reaping these benefits in the next hour—yes, I said hour—all you need is a blank composition notebook and a pen.

> **Author's Note:**
> This chapter is meant to give you an overview of the MAP Book method that I use. Check out my website for a step-by-step video tutorial on how to set up your entire system in sixty minutes or less.

What Is A Map Book, Anyway?

Busy moms need a system that they can trust to organize everything they have to do, everything they want to do, and everything they dream of doing. That is why I created the MAP Book. My MAP Book system, loosely based on the idea of a bullet journal, stands for my "Make a Plan" book. I've helped dozens of moms get theirs off the ground over the past two years. And I promise you, once you've customized this system to work for you, you will never go back!

This system is so mom-friendly because all you need is a pen and a 99¢ notebook. There are no hard and fast rules, and there is absolutely, under no circumstances, any calligraphy. I encourage moms to only invest 99¢ in their first notebook and, as soon as possible, make a mistake in it (scribble, cross something out, rip a page—I know, it stresses me out too). For some reason, knowing that your MAP Book won't be perfect from day one will help you develop and trust your system so much faster.

How a Notebook System Will
Accelerate Your Growth

A notebook organizational system is going to accelerate your growth faster than any other tool. Why? Well, first, you will never have to worry about forgetting something. If you think of something while you are reading before bed, you can grab your MAP Book and write it down. Because of this, your brain is not trying to remember every little thing. This will lead you to feeling generally less overwhelmed and more capable of thinking of the big picture.

How many times have you been at Target fifteen minutes before a birthday party starts? Let me guess, you swore up and down in the self-checkout line that next time, this wasn't going to happen. Next time, you are going to be more proactive. We've all been there, Mama! But how do you get more proactive? The second reason the MAP Book is awesome is that it does just that–it allows you to plan ahead rather than be reactive to what is happening in real-time.

Finally, a notebook system will keep you focused and confident about what is important. You will be able to identify what you need to do every day and what is a "want to do" versus a "have to do." Prioritizing tasks will be so much easier, and if you find yourself with a magical five minutes of free time, you will know exactly how you can spend it.

Utilizing Your MAP Book Daily

Now that you know what a MAP Book is, let me explain generally how I use it. Keep in mind: I have been doing this for about five years now, and a lot of these nuances have evolved over time. So, if you feel overwhelmed, simplify to what you need in this moment and allow yourself to grow into the space.

Weekly Pages

Each Sunday, I use two pages in my notebook to map out my week. I write down tasks in two major categories that I want to accomplish: my personal/family life and my work. In order to identify these tasks, I review my monthly pages, my monthly reflection wheel (more about this in Chapter Three), and my calendar. I consider this my "menu" for the week so that I can select tasks from it each day.

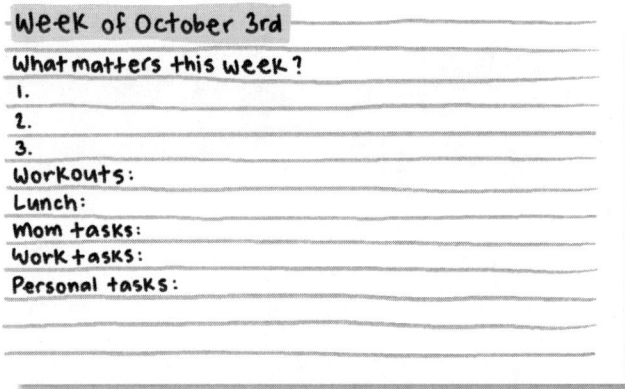

> **Week of October 3rd**
>
> What matters this week?
> 1.
> 2.
> 3.
> Workouts:
> Lunch:
> Mom tasks:
> Work tasks:
> Personal tasks:

Daily Pages

Every morning, I take five minutes to set up my daily page. Under the date, I write down three affirmations that I am focusing on, three goal activities that I am doing to make those affirmations a reality, three top tasks for the day, five things I am grateful for, and then general tasks that need to be completed that day. While this sounds overwhelming, I promise that once you get into the practice of it, it will be second nature to you.

October 3rd

My affirmations
- I am a present mom.
- I am an exceptional wife.
- I am in the best shape of my life.

Goal Activities:
- Girl dates
- Date night
- Liift 4

Priority Tasks:
- mini golf with daughter
- Marketing presentation
- Workout, Day 2

Gratitudes:
- A husband that makes me the perfect coffee every morning
- Being able to do my workouts in my living room
- Having a flexible schedule
- So motivated by yesterday's podcast episode
- A dry bed on a rainy day

Tasks:
- Call Mom
- make vet appt. for Lucy

This is a great place to remind yourself that your MAP Book pages, especially your daily pages, should align with what you need. Maybe you just want to write down your workout, the number of steps you want to take each day, three things that are stressing you out, and your to-do list. Go for it! If that is what makes the most sense to you, that is how you should format your daily pages.

Maximizing Your MAP Book's Potential

When you open my notebook, the first thing you see (on page one) is the table of contents. This is where I write down anything that I think I'm going to want to find again—notes about a book, notes from a meeting, brainstorming pages that I did, important lists. I create this table of contents as I go, and honestly, I only update it once every few weeks when I'm watching TV or waiting for my kids to wrap up their jujitsu class. When I first began my notebook system, I did not use a table of contents, and I would often find myself flipping endlessly through pages, looking for something that I knew "was there somewhere." The table of contents makes this process more efficient.

Monthly Pages

After the table of contents, the next three pages are my monthly pages: one for each of the next three months. Under each month, I list anything that I know needs to be done—think birthdays, anniversaries, vacations, holidays, etc. This provides you with a catch-all for any major to-do list items that are specific to the next three months.

Future Lists

After the monthly pages, my next section is for future lists. I currently have three future lists, but they usually change with every notebook. In this quarter's notebook, my first future list is things that I want to do in this current year. It is labeled "Things I Want to Do By The End of The Year." These ideas are things that I know I want to make happen, but maybe I am just not sure exactly when.

My second future list is my "Someday, Maybe" list. This was inspired by David Allen in his book *The Art of Getting Things Done*. On this list, I write down ideas that pop into my mind of things that I want to think more about or come back to later. I do not know if I am actually going to pursue any of these ideas, but it is nice to have a catch-all and, most importantly, to get them out of my mind and captured on paper.

Finally, the last future list that I have in my Q3 and Q4 notebook is a birthday/Christmas list. Remember how I told you that your MAP Book is a proactive tool? This is why! I write a quick list of all the people that I buy presents for every Christmas, and then throughout the year, I jot down ideas as they come to me. Trust me, I'm super thankful for this list every Thanksgiving! Other ideas for future lists could be: house projects that you want to tackle, seasonal bucket list ideas for family activities, books that you want to read, and recipes that you want to try.

> "If any part of the MAP Book set-up process feels over-whelming for you right now, skip it or make it work for you."

Random Lists

As a veteran MAP Book user, I have a variety of other pages. Whenever I read a personal growth book that I think I will want to reference later, I take notes directly in my MAP Book. Every quarter, I write my annual goals and quarterly goals in the back of my notebook so that they are an easy reference. When I find myself getting overwhelmed, I will often make a quick list of "Things That Are Overwhelming Me Right Now" and get everything out of my head.

If any part of the MAP Book set-up process feels overwhelming for you right now, skip it or make it work for you. Remember, you have permission to make this your own. And don't forget, be sure to check out the MAP Book set-up guide on the resources page of my website for a more visual walk-through of the MAP Book set-up process.

LET'S MAKE A PLAN!

- Get yourself a blank notebook and a pen.
- Download the free MAP Book set-up guide on my website.
- Have fun setting up your notebook!

Up Next

In Chapter Three, you will:

- Learn a system for regularly checking in with all areas of your life in five minutes or less a month.
- Prioritize action steps that will quickly lead to growth across all areas of your world.

CHAPTER THREE

Assessing Your Current Context

Beth, one of my coaching clients, felt stuck. On paper, she was living a life she dreamed of having back in college. She was happily married to a great guy, had two pre-teen kiddos, had a job that she was satisfied with, and generally felt like she had it all together. When we first sat down together, she told me, almost apologetically, "I just don't know where to go from here—nothing feels wrong!"

This, my friend, is a trap that a lot of busy moms fall into. They want to grow. They want to continue to improve their lives for themselves and their families. They're just not sure how to go about doing it. And they almost feel guilty for not having major issues to troubleshoot.

That is more than okay, Mama! Addressing your personal growth does not mean something is wrong with you or your situation. Even good things can get better. Personal growth doesn't mean you have to upend your life, divorce your spouse, write a book, start a podcast, or quit your job. It doesn't mean you have to homeschool your kids or buy a cabin in the middle of the woods...unless you want to. Personal growth is about making small adjustments to bring more joy to your life. Because we can all use more joy, right?!

When I first start working with a new client, the first component of their dream life that we discuss is what their current context looks like. After all, how can we move toward that dream life when we haven't taken a complete inventory of where we stand today? Like reading a map, you need to know where you are in order to navigate to where you want to go.

Using a Reflection Wheel To Figure Out Where You Are

The best strategy for assessing your current context is a monthly reflection wheel. To analyze where Beth currently was, we started with this reflection tool to examine seven categories of her life:
- Work
- Partner Relationship
- Parenting
- Personal Growth
- Recreation
- Exercise and Nutrition
- Physical Space

For each of these categories, I asked Beth to rank how she felt about that area on a scale of 1-10, with Level 10 being the best it could be and Level 1 essentially meaning it's not happening or needs a ton of work.

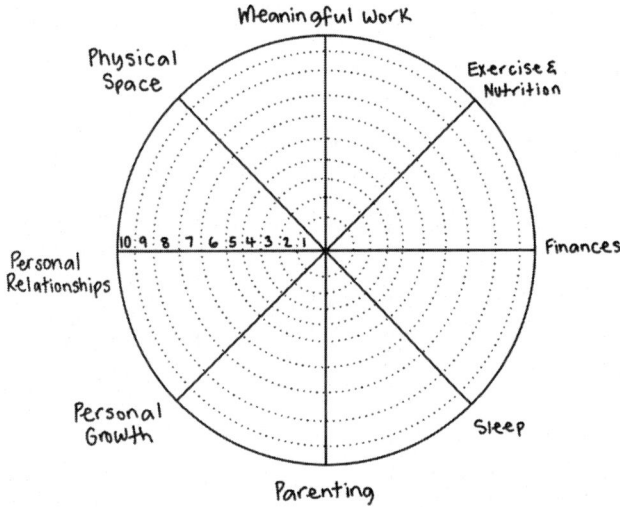

This exercise was eye-opening for Beth. When she connected the lines on her wheel, she was startled to see that her rankings for Partner Relationship and Personal Growth were much lower than the other categories were. After reassuring her that categories will ebb and flow at different times, we got to work to see how we could improve her Personal Growth and Partner Relationship over the next month.

The first step was to talk through each category and think about what she wanted the category to ultimately look like. For Personal Growth, at first glance, Beth felt like she really wasn't doing anything at the moment. Then we talked about podcasts that she was consuming and books that she was reading. She admitted that she used to be an avid reader in college but, since having kids, had unintentionally dropped her good reading habits. Even though her husband had given her a new Kindle for Christmas, she never felt like she had the time to just sit down with a book between working and shuttling her kids to after-school activities. That being said, she admitted that she missed that part of her life and would be open to regaining her good reading habits in order to further

39

her own personal growth.

Together, Beth and I brainstormed everything we could think of that was of interest to her for her Personal Growth category. This is the list we generated together:
- Create a list of books to read
- Order the books on Amazon/put on hold at local library
- Create a Goodreads account and connect with friends
- Set a goal for reading one book a month (any genre)
- Download an audiobook app from library and figure out how to use it

Beth was genuinely excited to get started with a physical book in her hands, but she acknowledged that her schedule wasn't getting less busy. With the goal of reading one book a month, she knew it might be more realistic to replace her podcast consumption with listening to an audiobook on the way to work. It was a small tweak, but one that excited her to invest in herself.

For her first book, Beth didn't even plan to read a personal growth book. In establishing the habit, she picked a popular book that her friends had raved about, telling her how suspenseful it was. She knew if she started it, she would be incredibly motivated to finish it. And the added bonus of being able to discuss it with her friends made it all the more motivating.

When I checked in with Beth two weeks later, she had already met her goal of reading one book a month and had actually read TWO books per month. When she had gone to download the audiobook app, she realized that her library card had expired, which meant she found herself at the library to get it updated. The bookshelf that contained the new titles enticed her while she was at the front desk, and she ended up leaving the library with three books that she was genuinely excited to read.

The second category that Beth had chosen to focus on was her Partner

Relationship. Similarly to many of her friends, Beth felt like the hecticness of her home life–running from soccer practice to a playdate, to the grocery store, then back to work already?!–meant she and her husband hadn't truly connected in weeks. Beth wasn't truly worried about the foundation of her relationship, but she knew that it could use a jumpstart.

Unlike many of their friends, Beth and her husband didn't have a close network of people around them that they could lean on when they needed support. Because of this, Beth and her husband had to get creative with time away from the kids.

Beth was stuck at first when we started brainstorming potential action steps. She knew a date night would be nice, but she wasn't sure it was something that was going to be a game-changer for them. Here is the list that we came up with:

- Check-in with husband about how he was feeling about where their partnership currently stood.
- Compare calendars to see if there was any time they felt they could use to connect.
- Discuss what "connection" actually means...to both of them! Is it a conversation? Is it a date without the kids? Get specific here!
- Reach out to a local babysitter's group to see if they could book someone to come to their home on a weekly basis.
- Make a list of things they wanted to do together, just never seemed to have the time.

Beth decided that she definitely wanted her husband to be a part of this conversation, so they planned to sit down the next night after the kids went to bed to discuss it. She texted me the next morning that their conversation had been a great success. Her husband had noticed the same lack of connection as well and was open to addressing it. They decided that every day at noon, no matter what the other person was doing, there would be a check-in text so that they were actively thinking of one another during the day. Beth and her husband also decided to start instituting morning coffee dates, with no phones, before they each went their separate ways for the day. She did say that her husband wanted actual date nights, and they were going to be actively looking for a local teenager who would be able to come hang out with their kiddos every Tuesday evening for a few hours.

In three weeks, Beth was able to take two areas of her monthly reflection wheel that felt stagnant and ramp them up with a conversation with her husband, a reading goal, and an action plan. Just imagine what twelve months of focused effort could change!

Your Reflection Wheel

There's something special about actually taking out a pen or a stylus and writing on this reflection wheel that I can't quite explain. On the surface, you might think, "Oh, I'm doing great this month. I don't even need to do the wheel!" But then you get into it and realize, "Oh shoot, I forgot I haven't gotten a good night's sleep in weeks, and my nutrition is a mess!" So don't procrastinate this process. It's going to be the most efficient way to shine the flashlight on what needs to be addressed. This is the best way to take action toward your dream life efficiently and effectively.

To start, I recommend printing out the monthly reflection wheel (you can find a blank template on my website). When I do this, I batch it and print all of them that I need for the whole year, so I only have to get myself to the printer once. I love to keep my monthly wheels in my MAP Book on the next available page so that I can constantly refer back to it throughout the month. Another benefit of doing this is that you can then look back on the month prior as well to see what kind of progress you made without having to hunt for your wheel. Be sure to add the wheel to your table of contents for easy navigation!

Historically, I try to do my reflection wheel the first week of every month. Do you have to do this? Absolutely not. Make it happen when it can happen, Mama.

Once you have your reflection wheel printed out, I typically tape it on the top of the next available MAP Book page. As a header, I write "September Reflection Wheel" and sometimes toss the date on there for good measure. Then, I use a pen to go through each category and rate it from 1-10 by drawing a circle on the corresponding line. So, for the Parenting category, if I lost my you-know-what at the bus stop this morning, felt like I was distracted all week by my phone, and found myself extra frustrated lately with my oldest daughter, I might draw my circle at Level 4 for Parenting. Things aren't on fire yet...but they're closer than not. Some months, I even write a little note in the margin of the wheel, reminding myself of why I rated it the way that I did: inconsistent bedtime routine for kids, need a new pillow to get better sleep, going to bed too late. This way, if and when I refer back to it, I can quickly remind myself why this was the rating I gave that category.

Then, move on to the next category. Rate how you feel there. Continue in this way until you've hit all ten categories. One of my favorite things to do is to whip out a ruler and draw a line between each dot so that I now have a crooked circle on my wheel. Sometimes, there are sharp peaks and valleys, and that is absolutely okay. I love to be able to see the visual of how I currently feel about my month. Like a wheel, you want the tires to be as even as possible so that it turns. Your task now is to figure out how you can make your wheel more even so there are fewer peaks and valleys and things will roll (generally) smoother.

Below the wheel, on my notebook page, I write the title "Action Steps." Then, I go back to each category above and write down one action step that I believe could increase my rating in that category for the following month. Let's think through an example.

Let's say your Work category was at Level 5. Your new boss is beginning to irk you with his micromanagement, your team is losing gusto, and deadlines have been creeping up on you lately. All that being said, you just got an awesome bonus for a deal you just made, you were able to leave work early two days last week to go to your son's soccer practice, and your new assistant is making some of the processes you used to dread much more enjoyable. Middle of the road, right?

The question is, what could you do—what action could you take—to make everything just a little bit better next month? Maybe you decide that your team needs an afternoon "off," where you can take them out to lunch and have some casual conversation to breathe life back into them. Or maybe you can ask your assistant to create a new workflow to help you manage deadlines that are coming up. Remember, these action steps don't need to be huge, massive changes. They can be small tweaks to help you improve your situation incrementally.

Let's look at another example. On your reflection wheel, your Physical Space rating was an eight. Overall, you are grateful for the home that you share with your family, even if it is a mess most of the time. The reason you rated it as an eight is that the linen closet in the hallway has been on your mind a lot lately. Every time you go in there, something falls off the top shelf and gets stuck in the door, or you can't find what you went in there looking for. Your kiddos clearly have been in there recently, and you put off having to grab anything in there since you know it will stress you out.

What would be a reasonable action step for this category? This is where I really encourage you to think small with your action steps. You don't need to take a day off from work to completely reorganize the linen closet...unless you want to! A more reasonable action step would be to go through one shelf a week to declutter what you no longer need. Then, next month, maybe you will buy baskets from Target to prevent future explosions. The following month, you may decide to label these baskets. Not everything needs to be done or fixed right now, and that's okay. Maybe you could even add this to your monthly list for an upcoming winter month when you know things will be slower and you will have the bandwidth to tackle this task. This reflection tool is all about slow and steady progress.

What if one category doesn't really need an action step this month? The short answer? That's awesome! Many months, you will find that certain categories are holding their own, and explicit action isn't really necessary. I caution you to notice if you are avoiding certain categories, though, since it's highly unlikely that a category would be a Level 10 multiple months in a row.

Once you have all of your action steps listed below your wheel, it's time to get them on the calendar. This is where a lot of clients falter. "Wait, I wrote 'buy a new pillow' on my action plan, but how do I put that on my calendar?" It's a great question! Take ten minutes to decide when all of these action steps are going to happen. Are you going grocery shopping on Saturday morning, and there's an Ikea right down the street? Perfect, that seems like a great time to grab a new pillow. Have you been meaning to go Halloween costume shopping with your oldest daughter? Add your pillow chore to the list for that day and physically write it on your calendar as an appointment. It's absolutely fine if you need to move the appointment, but at least get it on there so you don't do next month's wheel and have the same action item carry over. That is what you want to avoid!

If there is absolutely no way that the action step can be completed by the end of the month, don't be afraid to add it to your monthly list or even to a future list in your MAP Book. That is exactly what these lists are for, and you can breathe easier, knowing that you will come back to this task when you have the space to do so.

Identifying Your Level 10 Life

At this point, let's take a minute to dive into what a category being a Level 10 on the reflection wheel really means. To me, Level 10 is the highest ranking—meaning there is very little room for improvement, everything is as good as it gets, and not only that, but you are rocking it so well that you're even helping (and inspiring!) others.

Whoa, that's a high bar to clear! To be honest, the category that I only really ever feel this way about is the Personal Growth category. I regularly feel as though I am investing in myself daily (since I've made it a priority), and through coaching, I know that I am helping to elevate other moms to help them create a life they love.

> " Achieving a Level 10 is not realistic every month, and that should never even be the goal. "

The point of this reflection wheel is to take a moment to truly consider how you are feeling in different categories and to get a snapshot of your current context. Achieving a Level 10 is not realistic every month, and that should never even be the goal. My goal is to improve a little bit each month in each category, knowing that some months are going to be more challenging than others.

I tend to get a little competitive with myself, and some months, I add up my total number of "points" for the month and write it on the corner of the reflection wheel page in my notebook. Then, the next month, after

I complete the entire process, I compare the numbers to see if I have improved in a general sense. Every once in a while, I'm motivated to look category by category, especially if I want to be reminded of what I was doing when things felt good in a category. But more often than not, each month is treated as a stand-alone, and I keep my eyes looking forward to improving the future.

Achieving Your Level 10 Life

After I have been working with clients for several months, I encourage them to think about what a Level 10 category would look like. Take exercise for an example. If you were to achieve a Level 10 for your exercise one month, what would that look like? To me, that would look like:

- Daily workouts of thirty minutes or more, at least five days a week
- 10,000 steps a day
- Feeling comfortable in my clothes
- Encouraging a friend or family member to join me on a walk/run

Whew, that would be quite a month! Is it doable? Yes, for sure. But, could you see how maybe another area would probably lose out because of the extra effort in this category? This is why the reflection wheel is constantly ebbing and flowing, and it's important to not treat it as a report card of your life. If you're just using it to feed your reflection and goal-setting, you are on the right track.

Gaining Traction on Your Level 10 Life

When you first begin to implement the monthly reflection wheel, your first instinct may be that a lot of changes need to be made. This is absolutely normal and what most moms experience when they first begin to implement this process.

Here is how you combat that: focus on one or two areas that you think will

create the most traction for you the fastest. Why? First, because it will motivate the heck out of you. If you see one area of your life skyrocket, you
are going to be fired up to try it in a different context. Second, because
some of these categories are foundational and by having great success
in one area, you may trigger a domino effect of changes in another area.

For example, if you begin to focus on just your Exercise and Nutrition, you
may suddenly see huge gains in your confidence, your energy, and your
sleep. That can trickle over to your Parenting category, your Partnership
category, your Physical Space category, etc. By choosing a high-leverage
category like this, you can make small changes that will cause big results.

Remember, Beth chose to only focus on two areas. She did not try to
tackle all of the categories in the first month. By doing that, you are asking
for burnout, which will defeat the entire purpose of this reflection tool. So
take it one category at a time, one month at a time. You got this, Mama!

Being honest with your current context and where you stand, today is
one of the most important first steps to designing your dream life. It's
also one of the hardest steps to take because holding up that mirror isn't
always easy. During this process, especially, it is important to be kind to
yourself and know that progress is coming. By engaging in this process,
you are inviting positive changes to come into your life, but you have to
start somewhere.

Now that you have taken the time to assess your current context, it is time
to start thinking about your dream life vision. After all, before you can start
living your dream life, you need to know exactly what it looks like.

Curating Your Dream Life

I'll be the first to admit that the idea of a dream life vision sounds a little
out there for my taste. With that being said, it truly is the crucial first step

to creating a life you love. After all, how can you know you are living your dream life if you don't know exactly what that looks like?

In the personal growth realm, a dream life vision can mean a variety of different things. As busy moms, our dream life vision is generally going to include our families as part of the final vision. When some people create their dream life vision, they go all the way to lounging on a beach with the newest Elin Hilderbrand book, 365 days a year. Mom? Mom who? There's no mom here!

We're not going to quite go that far. Don't get me wrong, a book on a beach by myself sounds pretty dang lovely right now. But this dream life vision doesn't include your most important thing–your family.

So our version of the dream life vision is going to be a little more "feet on the ground," if you will. When I do this visioning process, I like to imagine that, for the most part, our income would generally stay the same (the work may change, though!), our family remains the priority, and I have about as much time in the day as I generally do now.

With all of those variables remaining constant: what would the best, most ideal version of your life look like right now?

But wait, what about reading books on the beach? This isn't to say that your dream life vision has no room for hanging in the sand. But maybe this isn't the central focus of your dream vision–maybe this is a byproduct of your dream life coming to fruition. With all that being said, now it's time to start thinking through what your dream life vision looks like.

Designing Your Dream Life Vision

When I was at the beginning of my own personal growth journey, I had a lot of trouble buying into this idea of a dream life vision. At the time, I was an overwhelmed mom, dropping my kiddos off at daycare to go to a job that I no longer felt passionate about. A "dream life" felt like a luxury that was out of my reach. My husband and I had student loans, we had a mortgage to pay, we had to be grown-ups and be miserable. That truly was my mindset and how we lived for many years.

Then, one day, I began to really consider what my dream life would look like. I knew I definitely wasn't living my dream life. But what WAS my dream life? I opened up my notebook and did what I do best–I wrote a list. At the top of the page, I just simply wrote "Dream Life" and what the year would be five years from then. Then, I wrote down every single thing I could think of that would constitute my dream life. I expected my dream life vision to be flashy and grand, but do you know what the biggest thing was that I couldn't get out of my head?

I wanted to get my kids on and off the bus every day.

That was it.

Now, realize that I had no idea HOW I was going to make this happen at this point. I had just gone back to full-time teaching after my final maternity leave, and I felt stuck because of my teaching degree, my husband's student loans, and our general finances. But this exercise finally felt like I had permission to just dream. I didn't have to worry about the how. All I had to do was identify what my dream life looked and felt like. To me, it was being able to meet the bus every day. I kept that image in my mind of being there to greet the bus and used that to slowly gain momentum as I went through the next three strategies that you are going to learn about in Chapter Four.

And now, today? I get my kiddos on and off the bus every single day. That big yellow bus coming around the corner is my daily reminder that the time I spent creating a dream life vision was not wasted. And I am so grateful that I started when I did so that I could have this time with my kiddos that everyone will remind you, you can't get back.

Just like my dream life started with a vision, yours will, too. Take the time to really imagine what the best version of your life could look like, down to the smallest detail. In Chapter Four, we are going to work through three exercises together that will really help you brainstorm what this alternate version of your life could look like. Before you know it, your dream life will be your real life, Mama!

LET'S MAKE A PLAN!

- Print off twelve reflection wheels so that they can be quickly and easily taped into your MAP Book at the beginning of each month.
- No matter what day it is today, take the time to tape in a reflection wheel and assess where you stand today in each category.
- Toss a date on the top and decide on two to three action steps that will help you make progress over the next month.
- Put a reminder on your monthly page in your MAP Book to come back to this exercise next month to see your growth.

Up Next

In Chapter Four, you will:
- Explore three exercises that will help you to define what your dream life looks like.
- Start making your dream life your real life by breaking down your vision into concrete action steps.

SECTION TWO

Designing Your Dream Life

CHAPTER FOUR

Creating Your
Dream Life Vision

Sarah's youngest daughter had just celebrated her first birthday when Sarah looked around and realized she was no longer excited about the life she was living. During pregnancy, everything was exciting. Milestones, new routines, and schedules—there was a lot to keep up with. But now that her family was settled into a comfortable routine, Sarah couldn't help but notice herself asking, "Is this it?"

The majority of my clients actually come to me at this stage of life. They have had their last child, and their maternity leaves are in the rearview mirror. While they are not necessarily unhappy with their lives, they feel overwhelmed by the idea that there are no longer any built-in, big milestones to be worked toward.

At this point in the book, you have a solid understanding of where you are today and why a dream life vision is going to be your road map to creating a life you love. But how does a busy mom go about creating that dream life vision? In this chapter, you are going to explore three exercises to help you turn your dream life into your real life. By the end, you are going to not only have a crystal clear vision for what your life could become, but you will start to brainstorm concrete steps that will get you there.

This is the exact process that Sarah and I worked through together. By the end of our work, I received the following text from her: "Just signed up for an equine psychotherapy course and decided to go back to school to get my LPC to practice outside of school. I'm so excited to be excited for what's to come again!"

Before we get started, remember to keep an open mind. The sooner you create your vision for your dream life, the sooner you'll be able to live it. Here we go!

Strategy 1:
Dream Life Vision Thought Download

There is something to be said about a good, old-fashioned thought download or journaling session. Go ahead and take out your MAP Book, or find another place where you can write your thoughts down and be able to access them later. In the notebook, across the top, write the date that is five years from now. Then, underneath the date, brainstorm your dream life vision. Who are you five years from now? What job do you have? What does your family look like? How do you spend your day? What kind of car do you drive? What kinds of clothes do you wear?

The more detailed you get with this exercise, the more effective it will be. If you can, set a timer for thirty minutes or longer to really force yourself to think through the details. When I first did this exercise, I got incredibly detailed, and now it's uncanny to see how many of these things are now a part of the life that I am living. And it hasn't been even close to five years yet!

Here are some things that are currently on my dream life vision list:
- Purchase a vacation home in Ocean Park, Maine
- Fully max out our retirement investments every year
- Be able to work remotely with my coaching business
- Go on a personal retreat to somewhere warm every winter

The reason that we start here is so that you can identify and clarify what you want. Without a vision in your mind, it is hard to take concentrated, focused action. Without this vision firmly in place, you will not have a barometer in which to measure your progress. Again, you are not worried right now about action steps. You just need to get specific about what your dream life vision looks like because it will be different for all moms.

Mind Map

Now, I am a list girl myself. But whenever I find myself struggling with this particular exercise, I shake it up by creating a mind map. As a former teacher, I have stashes of chart paper that I purchased back in the day for my classroom. I lay one of these out on the floor of my basement, crank my "Pumped Up Playlist" (creative title, huh?), and use a rainbow of Magic Markers to draw out where I want my life to be in five years.

In the middle of the chart paper, I write the year that will be five years from now. Then, from there, I draw circles of all of my roles in life: mom, wife, business owner, homeowner, writer, etc. After I have all of these circles created, I brainstorm what I want to be doing in each of those contexts five years from now, when hopefully I am living my dream life. Again, making these as detailed as possible is the secret sauce to really pulling out the things that are the most important.

Whether you decide to do a mind map or a list for this exercise, your end result will be a solid starting point for you to build your dream life action plan on.

Strategy 2:
Ideal Day Exercise

The next strategy that you can use to create your dream life vision is to design your ideal day. This is one of my favorite exercises that I revisit several times a year.

First, write down your typical schedule as time blocks in your MAP Book: 5:00 AM wake up, 8:00 AM kids on the bus, 9:30 AM work day starts, you get the idea. Don't worry about the nitty gritty here. Start from when you wake up to when you usually go to bed.

Next, look at the whole day as it currently stands and ask yourself: what would be the BEST version of this? What would be the dream life version of this? This is definitely the hardest part. If you can, try to remove the limitations of your job, your finances, relationship status, etc., and just allow yourself to brainstorm. Do you crave time to read every day? Maybe you want to have a daily coffee date with your significant other. Or maybe you want to snuggle your kiddo every night before bed and read a story together. Do you want to have modified work hours? Only to work a few hours a day? Decide what your ideal day would look like. Give yourself space to do this dreaming.

In other contexts, I usually encourage you to take this exercise one step further and see what life upgrades you can embed in your life now, realistically. For the purpose of creating your dream life vision, though, you don't necessarily need to take that step right now. All you are doing now is opening your mind to see what your dream life could potentially look like. We'll dive further into the idea of life upgrades in Chapter Ten.

Once you have envisioned how you would spend your time in your dream life, now you are ready to start tapping into some of the emotions that you want to feel once you have created a life you love.

Strategy 3:
Creating a (Dream Life) Vision Board

I saved the idea of creating a vision board for the end of this chapter because this is probably the most touted strategy on Pinterest. Yet, I would argue that it is the least effective for envisioning your dream life. When most people create a vision board, they think about THINGS they want to have: a new car, a huge custom-built house on the side of a cliff, a brand new Kate Spade purse. But are those really the components that make up your dream life?

Don't get me wrong, there was a time in my life when I was jealous of a friend who could just swing by the mall and pick up something from Tiffany's without batting an eyelash. But now? Now, I'm way more jealous of a woman who takes her kids on regular date nights and spends every Tuesday afternoon hiking in the woods with her dog.

All that to say, if you decide to use the vision board strategy to help you imagine your dream life, I suggest some parameters. First, use this as a secondary exercise. Meaning, do the heavy lifting with one of the previous exercises so that you can really dig deep about what that dream lifestyle looks like. Then, you can grab a pile of magazines or open Canva and get to work.

Second, push yourself to create a vision board that is a visual representation of the feelings you want to have when you're living your dream life. For me, my vision board is all about time freedom, flexibility, and financial independence. If you look at my vision board, you might see my time freedom represented by a towering stack of books that I have time to dive into and a blank calendar with a lot of white space on it. To represent my desire to feel rested, you might see an image of a wooden hot tub, a lake house, and an image of a beach at sunset. My desire for financial independence might be symbolized by a screenshot of a paid-off mortgage, an early retirement date, or a picture of a check to cover my children's college tuition.

To check and see if your dream life vision board represents the feelings you want, go through each image. What does it represent for you? How does seeing that image feel? If you don't feel a visceral response to that image in your body, it honestly doesn't belong on your dream life vision board. Ideally, you will look at your final visual representation and get sweaty palms or butterflies in your stomach.

Again, I absolutely do believe that a vision board is a great visual representation of your dream life vision. But use it just as that—a visual representation–not as an exercise to create your dream life vision. Otherwise, you're going to get stuck at your dream life vision on the surface level. That definitely won't lead to the fulfillment that you desire.

Making Your Dream Life Your Real Life

At this point, you have invested your time into creating your dream life vision. And now it's time to start making it your reality.

The thing that you need to know about me is I am all about the action steps. I can 100% buy into the idea of having a dream life vision. But, as soon as I've created it, I want to know what to do with it and how to take action.

Now, this is a double-edged sword of sorts. Remember earlier, when I promised you didn't need to worry about HOW you were going to do anything right now? That is still valid. You don't need to know how your dream life is going to turn into your reality right now.

That being said, you do need to commit to making an investment in your personal growth at this point. If you want to see your dream life become your reality, you will eventually have to take action. Notice that I didn't say swift action or immediate action. When it comes to creating your dream life vision, slow and steady is the best pace, so you have plenty of time to course correct along the way. Think of your dream life vision as more of your guiding star than of your lighthouse. The line won't be absolutely clear, but if you go slow and steady, you will stay on track.

Step 1: Identify What You Want
Good news! If you already completed the exercises above, you are well on your way to completing this first step. I had a mentor tell me once that creating your dream life vision is sort of like placing an Amazon order to the universe. If you are vague and unsure of what you want, you're more

than likely going to be disappointed. BUT, if you take the time to know specifically what you want to see in your dream life vision, it's more likely going to come into your life.

Think about my example of getting my kids on and off the school bus every day from Chapter Three. When I first identified this as something that I wanted in my dream life vision, I had no idea how it was going to happen. I was a full-time elementary school teacher who needed to be at school at the same time my kiddos would someday get on the bus. They were in toddler and infant daycare at the time, and I had no idea how I could make this my reality. Time was ticking!

But a few months after I identified this as something that I really wanted, I invested in a photography class, more or less "on a whim." Looking back, that was a pivotal point for me because photography gave me a way to leave teaching and make my school bus goal happen. I didn't know it at the time, but looking back, this was how I was going to make the school bus dream a reality.

Some people call it manifesting. Other people say it is calling your shot. No matter what you label it, I truly believe if you clarify what you want, you will find a way to make it happen. You will be more aware of and open to opportunities that will help you get to this goal. After all, you're a busy mom—you can do anything!

Step 2: Your Potential Steps

Now, some personal growth gurus will insist that once you've identified and clarified what you want, you can sit back and wait for the universe to deliver it to you like an Amazon Prime package. This is where I get off the manifestation train. While I fully believe this is a process that takes time, I also think action is required to make the change you want to see in your life. Our kids' childhoods are short. If I had spent ten years trying to manifest being home to put my kids on and off the bus every day, I may have missed my window entirely.

That being said, the second step for bringing your dream life vision to life is to begin to strategize and systematize the steps to get there. I strongly suggest choosing one aspect of your dream life vision and putting all of your focus on that for the time being.

Let's go back to the school bus example. When I first identified that as a cornerstone of my dream life vision, I sat down with my notebook and wrote that goal in the corner of my notebook. Then, I took a chunk of time to brainstorm everything that I could think of that would allow me to be home at 8:30 AM and 4:00 PM. Full-time teaching was out, but I could probably pull off part-time teaching financially. Added it to the list. I could start writing my book—added it to the list. Remembered I've always been vaguely interested in real estate, and then I could make my own hours. Added it to the list. Keep going like this until you have completely exhausted all options. Even if something feels ridiculous, write it down. It may trigger another thought later on that causes a domino effect.

Next, you want to take some time to make sure you have truly exhausted all of the options by doing some research. Enter Google. Set a timer for the amount of time you are committed to researching this to avoid going down any rabbit holes for too long. Search for ideas on Google or Pinterest that look appealing and could potentially help you get to your dream life vision.

Now this is the hardest part: walk away from this list. Seriously, I know you want to take immediate action and make things happen, Mama. But take a beat, put a reminder on your calendar to revisit this, and give yourself some space. You'll be surprised at how things may shake out. When I walked away from my list in November 2017, I didn't come back to it until March 2018. In May, a part-time teaching job opened up, which was very rare in my school district. Had I not made that list in November and had time to marinate in different options, I probably wouldn't have felt confident enough to jump on that opportunity.

After some time has gone by, revisit this list of potential action steps that will get you closer to your dream life vision. Now, start to take small steps. Do you know what you need to do to get your realtor's license? Take a few minutes this week to Google it. Not sure how much money you would need to bring in if you shifted to part-time work? Sit down with your partner to create a budget and decide the minimum amount you could comfortably get by on for a certain length of time.

I can't say this enough: this is your time to explore. Keep an open mind, experiment, and start to mentally prepare for a change because it's coming, Mama. Your dream life vision has been ordered. Just be careful you don't miss the delivery. This exploration could look like setting aside thirty minutes one night a week to poke around on Pinterest and explore new ideas to add to your strategy list. It could look like going out to coffee with a friend who is living aspects of the dream life you want. Or it could be meeting with a personal growth coach to help you focus your action steps and take action. There really is no right or wrong during this exploration process. It truly is about being open to what comes next, in whatever form that takes.

> **A WARNING:** At this point, I would be remiss if I didn't pause to give you this word of caution. At this point in the journey, when you start asking questions, doing research, and exploring possibilities, you may notice a shift in the energy of people around you. As humans, we are biologically programmed to be intimidated by the idea of change and growth. When one person begins to show discontent or a yearning for change, often that can bring up feelings in other people that are unexpected and can even be hurtful.

For many people, this deters them from making progress, and they retreat back to their former state. Don't be those people. Be a fierce mom who goes her own direction with confidence, knowing that you are creating a life that you would want your kids to have one day. The first time someone tries to knock you down from your path of change is super upsetting. Trust me, I've been there. The people around you who encourage the change and celebrate your progress are your community, though. Give them a chance to support you. And if they can't, find people who will. You do not need to give life updates to everyone in your world, and you sure don't need their permission to create your dream life.

Step 3: Strategize and Systematize

Now that you've taken time to explore all of the different options that are available to you, it's time to commit to some next steps, strategies, and systems. Again, this is where it is great to have a trailblazer who has already been down this path to guide you, but it is absolutely doable on your own if that is the road you decide to take.

Your goal at this stage is to decide on your strategy. What steps are you going to take to get you from where you are to where you want to be? For me, my first step was to invest in an online photography class. The thought of taking $500 out of our savings account made me nauseous, so I knew I needed a system to hold myself accountable for getting the class done. My fear was that a year was going to go by, and I'd remember about that course that I never took, just sitting in my inbox and wasting $500 that we really didn't have the wiggle room to waste.

The way to avoid that? Create a system. We're going to dive deeper into the idea of systems in Chapter Six, but for now, a system is a set of actions that you take consistently to achieve certain results. A strong example of that is the organizational notebook system from Chapter Two. Whenever a to-do list item hits my inbox, my kitchen counter, or my brain, it gets written in my MAP Book. That's my organizational system.

For my online photography class, my system was to wake up at 4:00 AM and spend an hour watching the class, taking notes, and learning my camera. While writing this book, my system was to write every day, from 6:30 to 7:00 AM, after my coffee date with my husband but before I had to wake up my girls for school. It's a system to make sure important things happen.

So, what is your system going to be for achieving your dream life vision? Let's say that your first step is to master your workout routine so that you can feel more comfortable in your skin in your dream life. Your system could be setting your alarm to go off every day at 6:00 AM and doing thirty minutes of yoga in your bedroom to start the day and establish the habit of working out first thing in the morning. Maybe then, a few weeks later, you change yoga to pilates then start training to run your first 5K. Creating a system to move you toward your dream life is for sure a challenging step. That being said, it is essential to be able to take consistent action–the secret sauce to successfully creating your dream life.

Step 4: Take Consistent Action

The majority of this process is fun and exciting: imagining the way your life could be, researching new paths to get you to your dream life, creating systems to get you there. But this step, taking consistent action, is the least sexy step there is. I truly believe that this is the breaking point for most moms who want to create change in their lives. They are able to decide where they want to go, create a system to get there, and then are defeated by the need for consistent action.

What is consistent action? Consistent action is taking daily action toward your dream life, even if it's the last thing you want to do. It's writing 500 words every day, even though you don't feel inspired. It can be cranking through a thirty-minute Hiit workout, even when it's a rainy morning, you were up last night with the baby, and you just want to sleep in. Consistent action is just what it sounds like: it's consistent, predictable, and happens no matter what.

This is the secret to consistent action toward living the life you are in love with: plan your system. Yup, that's it. Plan what your action is going to look like, and don't leave anything out. In Chapter Eight, you will learn more strategies for creating habits and systems that you can stick to.

Final Words about Consistent Action

Here's some real talk for you: this stage is going to be the longest stage on your journey. Dreaming, exploring, and planning are the fun parts. Implementing strategic, consistent action is where things get challenging. It can often feel like you're spinning your wheels and not seeing any real results.

Give it time, Mama. Be patient. The results will come. Think of this as a test from the universe. It's waiting to see if you can hang on. You can, and you will! Remember, little eyes are always watching. Be the person you want your children to grow up to be.

> "Consistent action is just what it sounds like: it's consistent, predictable, and happens no matter what."

Step 5: Align/Course Correct

After you have spent some time dreaming and scheming and implementing consistent action, it's time for the final stage: align and course correct. Check in with yourself—how are things feeling?

Let's say that you've decided to take a course in calligraphy because you want to open an Etsy shop for some side income. Your consistent action has been tackling this calligraphy course in twenty-minute increments on your lunch break at work. How is that going? Have you noticed any positive or negative changes? Do you look forward to that time investment, or do you dread it?

You want to be really honest with yourself at this point. If you discovered, three hours in, that you actually hate calligraphy, an adjustment needs to be made. On the flip side, maybe you LOVE the time you are spending on the course and are beginning to realize that if you spent more time on it, you would make more progress faster. Then, it may be time to revisit your system and make some tweaks so that you are investing more time in this venture.

In this stage, you want to constantly be going back to that idea of a dream life vision. Are the actions that you are taking moving you closer to that vision or further away? Again, this is a great argument for having a visual representation of your dream life vision that you see multiple times a day. It reminds you what you are working for and helps you check in to see if what you are investing your time in is helping you to spur progress or hinder it.

Some moms learn in this phase that what they thought they wanted wasn't actually all it was supposed to be. Maybe they start writing their novel in 500 words a day, and by the middle of the month, every day is a struggle, and they're dreading it. Or maybe they start training for a 5K and realize running isn't for them (or their knees!). This can be a hard reality to accept because this may be an identity that you've been looking forward to embodying.

By being honest with yourself here, though, you can make some educated decisions. Maybe the timing is wrong. Maybe running isn't for you, but could you try biking? When you love writing, but your novel is a train wreck, maybe you just need to tweak your idea or your genre or walk away from it for a month. This is also a good place to check in with an accountability partner or a coach to validate your feelings. If you have selected someone who is a good match for you, they should be able to hold up a mirror for you to help you (gently) see the reality of your situation.

While it's important to be realistic with yourself, it's also important to recognize that some progress is just slow. If you want to lose 100 pounds, that's not going to happen overnight. If you want to launch a business, there are so many steps to get that off the ground, it's not even funny (trust me, been there–done that!). Definitely consider if you need a new way to take action, but also trust the process and know that some paths to your dream life vision are going to be more of a marathon than a sprint.

You did it, Mama. As you finish this chapter, you have taken the first step toward living your dream life: deciding what that looks like for you and your family. Now, your next step is to think about how you could maximize the time that you have to start taking consistent action toward your dream life. You'll be glad tomorrow that you started today!

LET'S MAKE A PLAN!

- Complete the Dream Life Vision brainstorm in your MAP Book.
- Map out your ideal day in your MAP Book.
- Create a (dream life) vision board using whatever medium you choose. Plan to post it somewhere you can refer to it often.
- Practice walking through each of the five steps of making your dream life your real life.

Up Next

In Chapter Five, you will:

- Track your time to understand where it is currently going.
- Learn how to use the time you currently have to actually work toward your dream life vision.
- Get clear on what matters most during this season so that you can prioritize your energy to achieve your dream life faster.

CHAPTER FIVE

Time Maximization For Busy Moms

When I first met with Kaycee, the first thing that burst from her mouth was: "I know I should be doing more. I just have so much trouble waking up early when I'm up all night with the baby. All I want to do at night is collapse in front of the TV and scroll on my phone. I know I should be more productive. Help me!"

Take a second to re-read the name of this chapter. And, Mama, listen to me. I'm going to tell you the same thing that I told Kaycee. You have a lot going on. There are small humans that depend on you for their literal survival. I truly believe that any personal growth advocate who insists you need to make more time so you can do more things is causing more harm than good. You don't need more time. The trick is to take the time that you already have and make the most out of it.

The second caveat to the idea of time maximization is this: if you are in a hectic season of life, give yourself grace. I'm talking to you, mom in the back, who has a newborn strapped to her chest. This chapter–not for you. To the mom whose dad is in the ICU and has two toddlers at home–keep turning the page. This chapter is not for you...yet. It will be, but please give yourself patience and love and put all of your energy into surviving this season. Because you will, you always do.

This chapter is for any mom who is ready to get strategic about her days. That means you are likely getting a decent-ish amount of sleep, your family is not currently in crisis, and you have the bandwidth to make some meaningful changes. We are going to get into the nitty gritty about how you can maximize your time, be strategic with your energy, and make hard choices about what you spend your one life focused on. After all, without maximizing your time, you will not find the space to create and live your dream life.

Getting Clear On Your Time

In Laura VanderKamm's book *168 Hours*, she explores the idea of time management for moms. The premise of the book is that we all have the same amount of time–twenty-four hours a day, 168 hours a week. There's no way to make more time in your week. It's just about taking advantage and being thoughtful of the time that you do have.

One of the very first steps in the time maximization process is discussed at length in VanderKamm's book. In order to understand how you are currently spending your time as a busy mom, she suggests tracking your time for seven days to really understand where your time goes.

Time Tracker
I have done this practice for years now. Why? Because it works. When seasons change, life gets hectic, and things start falling through the cracks, it is a great way to reset and recalibrate your schedule and your calendar.

When I first tried this exercise, my oldest daughter was a newborn, and I was home in those early, early days of maternity leave. Looking back at that time log, I almost have to laugh. With a six- and eight-year-old now, my days look far different than they did back then. Long gone are the days of pumping, diaper changes, and weight checks at the doctor. Now my time is spent at the library, riding bikes, and going to parent-teacher conferences. That being said, I'm so glad that I have records of those times and the perspective to understand the vast differences in the various stages of motherhood.

So, how can you track your time? As I mentioned, I do this practice about once a year. I create a Google Sheets document and leave the tab open on my computer for seven days. Down the left-hand side, I write different times of the day in thirty-minute increments. As the day goes on, I pop in at every mealtime to add what I have been doing generally in each thirty-minute chunk. For example, if I was dusting and doing laundry from 4:30 to 5:00 PM, I would write "Home Management" in the box for that time slot. If I was reading with my daughter and then we went and played double solitaire, I would write "Time with oldest daughter."

Because I am a self-proclaimed overachiever, I like to color-code the boxes, too, so I can quickly see the different categories (mom, wife, work, home management, and self-care are my labels). Color coding also helps with adding up how much time I spend in each category at the end of the seven days. I'm sure there is some fancy-pants way to do that using Google Sheets, but I'm not there yet.

At the end of the seven days, I take a guess about how much time I spend on each category during a given week. The first few times I did this exercise, I was appalled at how much time I spent on my phone and watching TV. It was way more than I realized! I was also surprised at how much time I thought I spent at work versus how much time I actually spent at work. It helped me to see that I had more time than I believed and that a lot of it was being lost to the minutiae of the everyday. Realizing this helped me to make some meaningful changes to my schedule. It also helped me to strategize our family time with my husband and opened the door to that conversation.

Now it's your turn! Hop on over to my website and download your free time tracker sheet. From there, get started recording your daily activities. If you have a great memory, go ahead and add yesterday's activities to your time tracker. Since becoming a mom, my mind has been like a cheese grater, so personally, I would just start tracking from here forward.

Here are some caveats. Do not, I repeat, do not wait for a "normal week." If you haven't learned this by now, there is literally no such thing. Your kiddo will get sick at school, your dog will eat a sock and need emergency surgery, or your boss will tell you that going to New York is on the agenda for...tomorrow. Just dive in today and make adjustments as needed. For example, if you end up getting sick, don't track those days and just add an extra day to the end of your time-tracking stretch.

The second caveat is don't change your actions for the sake of tracking. If you normally collapse on the couch on Monday nights with a glass of wine and Grey's Anatomy, write it down and do it! This isn't being graded or shown to anyone, so be honest with yourself. Honestly, this is a waste of time if you're going to doctor the results. Live your normal week, write down your normal activities, and then take stock.

Once you've completed this exercise, take some time to add up the hours in each of your categories. Then, take some time to reflect on a few questions to consider how your time is currently being maximized:
- Where do I spend most of my time?
- Where do I spend the least amount of time?
- What categories surprised me (more or less time is spent there than you realize)?

After you understand how your time is truly being spent, it's time to dig deeper and continue to plan how you might want to spend your time in your dream life.

Identifying What You Need

When you are thinking about designing your dream life as a busy mom, your knee-jerk reaction may be to close this book and run away. As a mom, there are so many aspects of your life that are outside your ability to control (I'm looking at you, two-year-old, who doesn't consistently nap anymore!). Think of this section as a reflection exercise, even if you're not ready to commit to any action steps yet. It's important for you to decide what you want your ideal day/week/month/year to look like so you can (eventually) add some of these aspects into your day-to-day.

In Chapter Four, we dove deep into what a dream life vision looks like and how to create one. That is not what this chapter is all about. This chapter is about creating an ideal day/week/month/year in the actual life that you are living now. So, if you are working full-time with a one-year-old in daycare and a partner who works nights, you're designing the most ideal day for your life right now.

Things I Need Exercise
To start this reflection exercise, you are going to create a list on the next free page in your MAP Book. On this list, write the following subtitles: "Things I Need Every Day," then "Things I Need Every Week," "Things I Need Every Month," and "Things I Need Every Year." Now, take the word "need" with a grain of salt. Do I NEED thirty minutes a day to read my book? No, but I sure am cranky when I don't get that! List everything you can think of.

Here are some ideas to get you started with your own list:

Things I Need Daily:
- Cup of coffee
- To work out for thirty minutes
- At least ten minutes to read/be alone/recharge
- Shower
- Eight hours of sleep

Things I Need Weekly:
- Date night
- To be able to go grocery shopping without the kids

Things I Need Monthly:
- A chunk of time to check in with our budget

Things I Need Yearly:
- Time to budget for the year ahead

This list is a great thing to share with a partner or whomever you share your home with. I try to redo this list once a year so that it stays current (finding time to take a daily shower is no longer as challenging as it was when my daughters were first born, for example). I ask my husband to complete the same exercise on a date night, usually out loud, so we can both voice our needs in a neutral environment. This helps us to be empathetic with one another and truly understand what the other person needs.

Reimagine Your Time

Once you have decided what you need, it's time to start to envision what your ideal day in your current life might look like. Remember, this ideal day is going to be based in your current reality as much as possible.

When I do this exercise, I typically start with my "normal" schedule: what time I wake up, when the kids get on the bus, when my work day starts, when the kids get home, etc. This is not the place to get lost in the details. Give yourself permission to generally map out your day, from start to finish, in time blocks.

Next, I look at the whole day as it currently stands and ask myself: what would be the BEST version of this?

A few years ago, my family got hit with COVID. I got it pretty bad and was in bed for almost thirteen days. Our schedule after that was all off. Obviously, I was focused on recovering, but once I did, I had a chance to recreate my ideal schedule.

Once I was back to semi-normal, I was waking up with my kids at 7:00 AM. Then everyone was grumpy; we were already late, and at least one of us was crying when the bus rolled up at 8:15 AM. That was not my favorite.

So, I sat down with my schedule and created my ideal day. As a part of my ideal day, I would wake up at 5:00 AM, get to do my meditation, work out, have a coffee date with my husband, make progress on my life coaching certification class, and plan my day. That would all happen before snuggling with my girls as they slowly woke up. Doesn't that sound so much nicer? So much less chaotic! I carried this practice through the whole day, reenvisioning stressful and chaotic parts of the day to make them the best they could possibly be.

Once you have your ideal day laid out in time blocks, it's time to plan backward. How can you make these things a reality? What systems do you need to put in place? Obviously, waking up at 5:00 AM meant that I couldn't be up until 11:00 PM, so I made adjustments to my plan so the day flowed more smoothly.

When I realized I needed to wake up at 5:00 AM, I set a bedtime alarm to go off at 8:55 PM the night before so I would be able to get in bed by 9:30

PM. I set up an afterschool system so that my kids emptied their lunch boxes and backpacks right after school and put their shoes by the door so there were no last-minute scrambles in the morning. We put a bin of socks downstairs so that no one was running back upstairs for those at 8:14 AM as the air brakes of the bus squealed outside our house.

Now, this is an important note: you need to choose one practice that you can start TODAY to get you closer to your ideal day. Just one. Want to start waking up at 5:00 AM, but you're waking up at 8:00 AM now? Set your alarm for 7:30 AM tomorrow, next week for 7:00 AM. It's all about the baby steps. Start layering in the next step when you get another part down pat. Keep this Ideal Day Schedule in your MAP Book for easy reference!

> "You need to choose one practice that you can start TODAY to get you closer to your ideal day."

I try to do this Ideal Day Schedule exercise once a year or whenever our schedule gets way out of whack like it did after COVID. This exercise helps me to focus on my priorities and keep my goals on track. In its simplest form, you are taking your schedule and asking yourself the question: what could I do to make it better? I promise you, you're going to have so much fun with this process!

An Ideal Day Example

In case you're like me, and an example always helps, I'm including my current ideal schedule. Does this happen every day? Heck no. Maybe one day a week looks exactly this way. But you know what? That day is super awesome, and the other ones have enough pieces of the ideal that they're pretty great, too.

So here's a peek into my daily life:

5:00 AM – morning routine
7:00 AM – wake up kiddos, breakfast, cleaning task
8:00 AM – bus, hope for the day with the kids
8:30 AM – clean up the kitchen, prep for work day
9:30-11:30 AM – work block
11:30 AM-12:00 PM – walk outside or on treadmill
12:00-12:30 PM – lunch
12:30-3:00 PM – work block
3:00 PM – catch up time with my husband
3:30-4:15 PM – time with our youngest before the bus comes with our oldest
4:15-5:00 PM – family routine time (library, game night, taco prep, kid dates)
5:00 PM – dinner prep & screen time
6:00 PM – eat dinner together
6:45 PM – learn Spanish together with Duolingo
7:30 PM – read Harry Potter together
8:00-9:30 PM – parents' time

When I was going through old copies of my MAP Books from previous years, I found my Ideal Day exercise from 2016. This is when I had a ten-month-old daughter and was working full-time, teaching fifth grade. Some things were similar, but a lot of things were different too:

5:00 AM – wake up, get dressed, pack for daycare, set up crockpot meal
6:00 AM – wake up baby, get her ready
7:15 AM – turn on crock pot, leave for daycare
8:00 AM-4:00 PM – teach and prep for next day
4:30 PM – daycare pick-up and playtime
6:00 PM – dinner
6:30 PM – baby bedtime (man, I miss that!)
7:00-9:00 PM – house chores, showers, pick up the house, prep bags for tomorrow

To be honest, this frantic schedule that prioritized work is actually one of the reasons I began to realize that I wasn't living in alignment with my dream life vision and started making big changes to match my priorities to my daily activities. Exercises like that helped draw attention to the dichotomy and laid the foundation for the creation of my dream life.

Getting Clear On What Matters in This Season

Whenever I read a time management book written by someone who isn't currently in the throes of parenthood, I can't help but shake my head. So many of the principles and ideas are just not feasible for parents who are trying to simultaneously accomplish so many things.

So, instead of stressing about how you are managing your time, this section is about maximizing the time that you already have. This time maximization strategy came to me from Kendra Adache of The Lazy Genius podcast. If you haven't heard of her, definitely check her out. I frequently recommend her to my coaching clients, and they are always as impressed with her as I am.

So the strategy is this—brace yourself for how simple this is: name what matters. That's it. That's the strategy. Name what matters. Why is something so simple, so profound? Let's dissect it a little bit!

When we think everything matters an equal amount, we panic. As moms, we know it's literally impossible to give everything our full attention. That's where overwhelm comes in. But, if instead of believing that everything matters as much as the next thing, we identify what matters MOST, we can redirect our energy. Let's see this is in action with an example...

When I was looking at my calendar for September, I was immediately overwhelmed. It's my photography busy season. I have a big website project that I want to complete, a full roster of coaching clients, AND it's back to school for both of my kids and my husband, who is a teacher. Overwhelmed is an understatement.

But when I forced myself to hit the pause button, I took my MAP Book and wrote down the four weeks in September—September 5th/12th/19th/26th. From there, I put two bullet points under each week and wrote down two things that mattered that week.

The first week of September? The things that mattered most were back-to-school routines and getting a bunch of editing done. That was it. That was all that really mattered. So, when I went to plan my day, I looked back at what mattered and made sure anything related to those priorities happened first.

The second week of September, I knew we would be a little more settled into routines, but the kiddos only had a four-day school week, so I wouldn't have a ton of time to work. So, I named what mattered in the second week as completing my website project and being present with my kids on their day off. If nothing else happened that week, that was okay, but those were the priorities.

Every week, when I sit down to plan the week out, I rewrite my priorities for the week from this list. It helps keep me centered and helps me feel like I am being proactive. Of course, some weeks are harder than others, and sometimes more than two things matter. But I always know what my big two are and can communicate them to my husband as well, so we're all on the same page.

How to Plan When You're Overwhelmed

While September can be pretty overwhelming, there are other spots during the year that I can point to on January 1st and promise you are going to be overwhelming and stressful. For me, they are the end of the school year, the transition to summer, the day before we leave on vacation, the day we get back from vacation, back to school, busy season, and all of December.

That is why this strategy helps so much because you can be proactive about these stressful times and backward plan to set yourself up for success. For example, I know that the first three weeks in November are going to be crazy stressful. I photograph all of my holiday mini-sessions in those weeks, and my photography clients are eager to get their images back so they can order holiday cards.

To be proactive, I sit down with my husband in October, and we decide what we can do together to overcome the overwhelm. He knows that he is the point person at home, and I usually try to do some meal prep ahead of time so he's not having to cook every night. I put editing days on my calendar so I'm not tempted to book a session during that time. I also carefully consider any social events during those three weeks since I know I won't be able to be fully present with friends and family until the work is off my plate.

Again, does this make November sail by without a hitch? Absolutely not. It just helps me feel proactive and more confident going into it. Imagine if I just woke up one day and said, "Oh shoot, I have ninety-five sessions to edit by tomorrow!" That would be overwhelming and pretty cruel to do to myself. So, I do what I can to get ahead of it and maximize the time that I do have.

Even if your life does not involve a busy season, per se, think of times of the year that you know will be harder than others. For example, maybe your busy season is back to school, the start of summer, or the holiday season. Give the future version of you the gift of planning ahead for success.

Becoming More Present With Your Loved Ones

More and more clients are coming to me with a similar concern: they feel like they are now maximizing their time with their families. However, they struggle to actually be present when they are with their children. Even if their phones are away, their mind is racing, thinking of the next thing that needs to be tackled, plans for the next day, or how long that chicken has been in the refrigerator.

I can't help but point to COVID here. Before the lockdown of 2020, many people, myself included, never dreamed of working from home. I was a teacher, for goodness sake! But when we were all of a sudden forced to turn our bedrooms into home offices and hide from our kids to get spreadsheets done, a shift happened. Even years later, I believe we are still trying to recover from this. Our work life began to overlap with our home life, and that is a hard mindset to overcome. So, if you are struggling with this, you are not alone!

Before we tackle how to overcome those distractions to be more present with your family, I feel the need to remind you of this. You have a lot on your plate. Being 100% present 100% of the time isn't always realistic. Give yourself some patience and grace. Let's explore five tips and tricks to make sure that you are getting the present time that you want and need with your kids:
- Set Clear Expectations
- Manage Technology
- Do A Thought Download
- Set Aside Time On Your Calendar
- Be Honest With Yourself And Your Child

Strategy #1: Set Clear Expectations
The first strategy for maximizing your present time, specifically with your children, is to set clear expectations for them. You might let them know that you will be able to play Uno with them for thirty minutes, and then

you have to start dinner. Depending on the ages of your children, you may want to set a timer or give them warnings. Personally, I prefer to set a timer. That way, I don't keep glancing at my phone to see how much time is left. You know how that goes: you check your phone to see the time, there's a text message that came through, and poof! You are instantly distracted.

Strategy #2: Manage Technology
Speaking of phones, whenever I strategize present time with busy moms, I encourage them to leave their phones in the other room, ideally on Do Not Disturb mode. A study done by Skowronek, Seifert, and Lindberg in 2023 suggests that the mere presence of a smartphone in the same room that you are in leads to a reduced attention span and lower cognitive function. If you truly want to be present with your kiddo, get your phone well out of reach and out of the room.

Strategy #3: Do A Thought Download
A third strategy for ensuring that you are mentally available to be present with your·child is to take a few moments before you give them your full attention to write down anything that is on your mind. I usually bring a sticky note and a pen with me when I'm trying to spend time being present with my kids. If I think of something that has to be done, I write it down instead of letting it distract me. This ensures that it gets transferred to my MAP Book and not forgotten so I can turn my attention back to my kiddos.

Strategy #4: Set Aside Time On Your Calendar
We're going to dive deeper into positive habits in Chapter Nine, but being present with your children is just another habit that you need to create. I recommend even putting the 1:1 time on your calendar so you are more likely to stick to it, like an appointment. After a while, you won't need to do this anymore, but it will help to train you to be present during these 1:1 sessions. My husband and I made a commitment this year to do at

least one 1:1 session a week with each of our daughters. We were able to agree that thirty minutes felt like the right amount of time. Wednesday afternoons are set as our 1:1 time together. Now granted, during certain seasons, this is more challenging than other times. But having it on the calendar helps us to prioritize (and remember!) to invest this time with our kiddos.

Strategy #5: Be Honest With Yourself And Your Child

And finally, my last tip for maximizing the time you spend 1:1 with your child is to be honest with the activities you are willing to participate in versus not. It helps to ask your child ahead of time how they want to spend their time together. If they suggest an activity that you dread (I'm talking to you, slime), don't be afraid to put a limit on it or suggest a different activity. Your 1:1 time shouldn't be spent watching them play a computer game. For me, I am not a fan of pretend play. I will do it occasionally, but I hesitate to sign up for thirty minutes of playing house every Wednesday. I clearly communicate that to my daughters and then suggest another activity that we could do together that we will both enjoy more. Again, that's not to say we can never play house—I just don't want to do it every time.

By setting a timer, creating clear expectations, and providing yourself with a tool to record random thoughts that pop into your head, you will be more present with the time you have with your kids. This is a time that you can't ever get back, and you will never regret investing. Remember to plan an activity that you both enjoy, get your phone out of the room, and add this time as a recurring event on your calendar to be as present as possible with your children.

Busy moms do not need more time. Instead, they need to maximize the time that they do have to strategically create their dream life. After completing the exercises in this chapter, you may notice that you are feeling overwhelmed with the sheer amount of things you want to do in a given twenty-four-hour period. Take a deep breath, though, Mama. This does not all have to happen at once. Take your time. Take what you need. You got this.

LET'S MAKE A PLAN!

- Track your time for one week using the time tracker on the website.
- Complete the Identifying What You Need exercise.
- Map out what your ideal day would look like.
- Make a list of What Matters in This Season and refer to it often.
- Choose one strategy for being more present with your loved ones.

Up Next

In Chapter Six, you will:
- Identify the core values that you want to live your life by.
- Learn how to align your regular activities to prioritize the things that are most important to you.
- Use your core values as a filter to help you make important life decisions.

CHAPTER SIX

Living In Alignment With Your Core Values

When I first started working with Cassidy, she was all over the place. We discussed a ton of new directions at our first meeting. Then, when we reconvened, she felt disconnected from all of them. Frustrated, she wasn't sure where to go next.

That is when I suggested that we focus on identifying what was most important to her: her core values. She immediately sat up higher in her seat and looked reinvigorated. "You know," she said, "I think that might be exactly what I need! I feel like I am always holding myself to what everyone around me thinks is important. It's my turn!"

When you close your eyes and envision your dream life, how much are your core values present? How well are you living in alignment with your core values right now? You could be 100% aware of your current context, be organized, have a vision for your dream life, and maximize your time every day, but if you aren't in alignment with your core values, not much is going to change.

Hold up, hold up, hold up. Are you able to identify what your core values even are? If you aren't, you're not alone, Mama! I operated for many, many years before I really decided to do a deep dive into my values to realign my lifestyle. Now that I am crystal clear about my five top core values, it is so much easier to say no to things that are not in alignment with who I want to be and prioritize the activities that are.

Defining Core Values

A core value is the essence of who you are. It is a trait that you feel passionately about. Without your prioritization of that trait, you wouldn't be the person that you are today. So what values are most important to you? What traits encompass who you are as a person? Identifying these values is harder than you might think!

Core values are often utilized in the business world as a part of a company's vision or mission statement. But as moms and as individuals, we need to identify our own core values in order to truly be in alignment. And when we can strategize to have our core values align with our dream life vision? Winning!

Why Core Values Matter

Before we really walk through the process of identifying your core values, it's important to identify how this process will help us. As busy moms, we don't need busy work. We need meaningful activities that will lead us forward and efficiently accelerate our growth. The reason it is helpful to identify your top values is because then you can start to create your dream life action plan around these values.

When we don't identify exactly what's important, then everything is important. And in the case of personal growth, that's just not true. Just like with time maximization, we want to make sure we are investing our time and energy in the right places.

In order to create an action plan to move yourself toward your dream life, you need to know what core values you prioritize above all others. Our values may change a little bit over time, but for the most part, they are going to stay the same. By identifying the most important ones, we can then dig deeply into the development of those values rather than just hitting the surface of dozens of important aspects of our personal growth.

When you identify your core values, what you really are doing is imagining the highest version of yourself. None of us can live in alignment with all of our core values at a Level 10 every single day. This work is about identifying what your core values are and then working to close the gap between where you are today and where you ultimately want to be.

Finally, and arguably most importantly, by knowing your core values, you can communicate them to others. That's not to say that you need to get a T-shirt with your top five on it, but when your significant other or children are aware of what is most important to you, they can help you stay aligned with those values. In addition, the whole point of personal growth is to create a life that you want your children to have. Don't you want them to live in alignment with their values? I certainly do! By exploring your values, you are taking the first step to modeling this process for them.

Strategically Living Your Core Values

Identifying your core values is a fruitless exercise if you don't take the next step to actually incorporate these values into your everyday life. By implementing these three action steps, you will be well on your way to living in alignment with your values every day:

- Complete a Value Assessment
- Create Your Mission Statement
- Revisit Your Dream Life Vision

Step 1: Complete A Values Assessment

Your very first step in this process is to obtain a list of core values (I have provided a PDF of the list that I use on my website. This list has 100 values, enough to really be able to shop around but not too many that you'll be paralyzed by the options, I promise! You can also search Pinterest or Google for a list of core values and use that. The list doesn't matter. The process does).

Once you have procured your list, it's time to get down and dirty! Grab a pen and go through the list for the first time. Cross out any values that you don't feel are very important in your life. If you're using the list that I provided for you, you will likely be crossing out about thirty values, leaving you with twenty or so that you feel positively about. Next, go through the remaining list and circle your top twelve values. This is where things start to get challenging.

After you've done that, I suggest writing the values you have left in your MAP Book so you can refer to this list later. When I did this exercise with Cassidy, we found that a lot of these values overlapped at this level. For example, Cassidy had "dependability" and "trustworthiness" as two of her top twelve values. Those words are pretty synonymous, so I encouraged her to decide which way she leaned more. In Cassidy's case, we actually realized that it's not really either of those words, but the idea of "loyalty" was more profoundly aligned with who Cassidy wanted to be.

This is a process, for sure. Don't be frustrated if you can't seem to narrow your list down. While you absolutely can do this in one sitting, you may need to step away and come back to it with a fresh mind and fresh eyes. When I did this the first time, I was bound and determined to walk away with at least a draft of my top five. So once you have determined your top twelve, it's time to narrow that down to your top five.

Here are some examples of questions you could ask yourself to narrow this list down:
- What was important to me as I look(ed) for a partner?
- How would I want to describe my grown children? What values do I want them to have?
- At my funeral, how would I want people to describe me?
- As a child, what was important to me?
- What kind of person do I want to be?

Now, some coaches will encourage you to take the list of your top five values and narrow it down one more time until you get your top three. That's not me. I personally feel as though five values is just the right amount. I can clearly remember them; they encompass most of my life, and most of my activities align with them.

Here is my final list:
- Growth
- Simplicity
- Alignment
- Meaningful work
- Relationships

While these are absolutely not all of what represents who I am, these are my priorities. Having them identified means that I can be more purposeful about including them in my life. In addition, I can communicate them to people around me to help strengthen my relationships as well.

Step 2: Create a Mission Statement
Whew, congratulations! That exercise is not for the weak, that's for sure. Now that you have identified your list of top five values, the next question

is: now what do you do with them?

My first recommendation is to sit on them for a minute. Share them with a partner, a friend, or a coach to see if they see those values mirrored in you. Occasionally, there will be one or two values that you want to embody but that you don't embody...yet. That is more than okay. It is actually ideal because you will work to strengthen those values with the action plan that we're going to start to create at the end of this chapter.

Once you have given your top five values time to breathe and you're confident that you have selected the most representative ones, it's time to put them to work.

These top five values are now going to turn into your personal mission statement and potentially even your family mission statement. In the first personal growth book I ever read, The Seven Habits of Highly Effective People, Stephen Covey shares the idea of creating a personal mission statement. It took me a while to buy into the idea, but then I realized that by creating a mission statement, I would have a filter to channel all decisions through. If I had an opportunity or a decision to make, I could consider this statement and my values to make the right choice for me (and, ultimately, my family). I am generally an indecisive person, so the thought of creating my own filter excited me.

Take a day or two to sit with your five values. Really take the time to think them through, maybe even brainstorm some ideas next to each value about why they are important to you. Then, turn each value into its own sentence.

Here are the examples from my list:
- Growth: I value growth above all else and continually work to improve my life and the lives of others.
- Simplicity: My life is centered around simplicity of pro-

cesses, material items, and routines.

- Alignment: I live in alignment with my values every day.
- Meaningful work: Having work that motivates and inspires me is more important than how much money I make.
- Relationships: I will always actively prioritize relationships with people who value me.

From here, you can guess the next step. Now, can you turn these sentences into one mission statement? Remember, this isn't a ninth-grade English class. If you prefer to keep the sentences as is, go for it. For me, it seemed like an overwhelming list, so I challenged myself to condense it. Here is where I landed:

I prioritize <u>my growth</u> and the growth of others over all else. Every day, I live in <u>alignment</u> with my values by investing my time in <u>meaningful work</u> and a <u>simple lifestyle</u>. I choose to prioritize and invest my time in <u>relationships</u> that are fulfilling and reciprocal.

Like anything, this mission statement is forever evolving. This isn't perfect, but it is a great reminder of my values and my purpose. I am confident that this statement will evolve over time, but for now, this feels like a good starting point.

At this point, if you've done all of this work in one sitting, I would encourage you to step away from it for a while to gain some clarity and perspective. Write this mission statement once a day in your MAP Book for a few days to see how it fits. You may find yourself unintentionally tweaking it, noticing gaps, or wanting to expand in certain areas. Allow yourself to do that. You have permission.

Once this mission statement feels aligned with you and your priorities, this is when you can share it with others that you trust. For me, it was important to share this with my husband. I loved the conversation that it ignited as we discussed our top values and thought about the implications that those had on our family. My husband's values are similar to mine, but he had some distinctly different values that I agreed I also wanted to pass on to our children. From there, we had a great conversation about how we could identify our family values and create our own family mission statement.

While a mission statement can feel like something just big companies do, consider the value of including it on your dream life journey. Your mission statement, just like your core values, can be the essential ingredient to the roadmap of your dream life.

Step 3: Revisit Your Dream Life Vision

At this point, you have identified your top five values, created your personal mission statement, and maybe even a family mission statement. That's a lot! You are well on your way with your personal growth journey, and I think this next step is going to tie a lot of loose threads together for you in the best way possible.

Remember that dream life vision that we created together in Chapter Four? Do you see your values reflected there? Take the time to pull out your MAP Book and flip back to your brainstorm for your dream life vision. Can you label each of these items with your values?

For example, my dream life vision might look something like this:
- Putting my girls on the bus every day – **relationships**
- Coaching busy moms to create lives they love – **growth/meaningful work**
- Spending our summers at a lake house – **simplicity**
- Going on a personal solo retreat somewhere warm every winter – **growth**
- Not working full-time hours – **alignment**
-

Do not be discouraged if everything doesn't line up as neatly as it does above. When Cassidy and I completed this exercise together, she had a lot of activities that were not in perfect alignment. Use this as a check to make sure this truly is part of your dream life vision, though. A lot of times, when you start to veer away from your core values, that is a sign that things may need some tweaking.

Step 4: Consider Who You Want To Be

If you are feeling confident about your dream life vision, I have exciting news for you: you're just about ready to start to create your action plan.

Your next step is to choose one of your core values. When you think about your dream life vision and what it would look like to embody this value every day, what does that look like? What actions will you take? What actions will you not take?

Don't rush through this exercise. Take some time to reflect in your MAP Book, then revisit your reflection. Add to it, make changes, refine it. Ideally, by the end, you will have a clearer picture of the person that you want to be. The more detailed that you can make it, the better.

For example, I want relationships to be the value where I focus most of my energy. I want to have strong, deep ties with my family, and I want to provide them with a calm, loving presence that they want to remain connected to. At the end of my life, I want to be someone that my grown children come to spend time with because they want to, and I want future generations to speak of me fondly. This aligns closely with my values of relationships and simplicity.

So from there, picturing that future version of myself, it's time to work backward. What could I do now to help achieve that future version of myself?

Here's a list of ideas that I brainstormed to get me closer to that dream life vision:

Want deep relationships with kids now
- Be present when home with them
- Weekly 1:1 dates
- Quarterly 1:1 trips (ideally overnight)
- Constant communication, even about hard topics–start this early
- Always be someone they can confide in

Shared experiences as a family
- Plan with the future in mind for holidays, family traditions
- Annual summer trip to Ocean Park, Maine
- Lakehouse

For right now, your core values are going to be an important aspect that you spend some time reflecting on in your life. In Chapter Twelve, when you begin to develop your dream life action plan, these core values are essentially going to be the pillars around which you organize your plan. Because of that, you want to ensure that these core values truly are the right fit for you.

Give them some air, some time to breathe. Put a note on your monthly page in your MAP Book to look back on this. Journal out some ideas or ask someone you trust to reflect on these values with you. The more confident that you are about the strength of these values, the easier it will be to create an action plan that you love.

LET'S MAKE A PLAN!

- Download the list of core values from my website to help you define what your top five values are.
- Use these core values to write a mission statement to be your GPS on your dream life journey.
- Revisit your dream life vision to ensure that your core values are represented.
- Decide on new activities that will help you live more in alignment with your core values.

Up Next

In Chapter Seven, you will:
- Get everything out of your head by doing a thought download.
- Learn how quarterly and weekly check-ins can help you be strategic and consistent.
- Be inspired to plan your year by focusing on five key steps.
- Explore the idea of going from twelve-month goals to twelve-week goals.
- Learn the best way to set goals when you are feeling overwhelmed.

SECTION THREE

Start Living A Life You Are Obsessed With Today!

CHAPTER SEVEN

Goal Setting For Busy Moms

When I first met with Tania, she shared with me that she wanted to be more proactively working toward her goals each day. Like a lot of moms, Tania felt like others around her were able to accomplish more, and she was spinning her wheels. Admitting that you feel constantly overwhelmed, yet never truly productive, is a common struggle that so many moms experience.

At this point in your journey, you have taken the time to get organized and have taken an honest look at your current life as a mom. You have a sense of what your dream life looks like, know that you need to maximize your time, and live in alignment with your core values. So, how does that translate into setting goals that will help you to achieve your dream life?

Before you can truly begin to make progress toward your dream life vision, you first need to establish a system for goal-setting that will help you focus on what really matters. Similarly to time maximization, you don't need to make more time or wake up at 4:00 AM (although you can!) or find a new schedule on Pinterest. You need to take the time that you have and align it with your core values and your dream life vision to make sure that the right action steps are being prioritized. Because this isn't a super simple process, it's something a lot of moms avoid doing. Thus, the feeling of being underproductive.

Let's dive into Tania's story a little bit. Tania is a top-level executive and works from home. She has a gorgeous 1700s farmhouse that they recently renovated, a supportive husband, and two kids—her oldest just entering kindergarten. She shared with me that she feels like she doesn't breathe or blink all day as she blindly cranks through her to-do list. Then, when her family arrives home after their day, she is just a puddle. All of her good intentions of getting the laundry done during calls and getting ahead on planning her son's birthday party are practically laughable by the end of the day. And forget having time to invest in the goals that she wants to focus on so badly. What's a mom to do?

These strategies will help you to make space for your goals and help you establish routines that will help you reach your goals more efficiently and effectively.

Getting It All Out Of Your Head: Brain Dump/Mind Sweep

The first step that I often recommend for moms who don't feel alignment in their never-ending to-do list is to complete a thought download. Often called a "brain dump" or a "mind sweep" in the personal growth realm, this is a popular strategy for truly emptying out your brain. The reason you do this is so that you can create space to focus on your goals by knowing exactly what needs to be done in other areas of your life. This strategy will help you to identify what is most important, so you are not running around putting out fires and doing random tasks that aren't truly the priority just because they are on your mind.

To do this, I recommend grabbing a legal pad and a pen. This is the one thing that I don't actually put into my MAP Book because of the way we're going to strategize it later. Make sure that you have at least an hour to complete this process, and, ideally, find a time when you are at the location where you want the thought download to take place. For example, when I was teaching and feeling overwhelmed at work, I would need to download my thoughts in my classroom. Sitting in my living room and trying to complete this effectively didn't work since I wasn't in the appropriate setting where I was feeling overwhelmed.

Next, set a timer for thirty minutes and start by physically walking around your space. On the legal pad, write down any to-do list item that pops into your head as an action step with a verb in front of it.

Here are some examples:
- Donate 3T clothes
- Ask husband to clear off his dresser
- Buy new socks
- Call dermatologist to make annual appointment
- Get quote from cleaning company

If you are focusing on your home, I recommend going into every room of your house, walking the exterior of your house, opening cabinets and closets—go all in. This visual process will really help you to get everything out of your head. By the time you have finished going through every space, you will feel confident that your list is thorough and that you won't open a cabinet tomorrow morning and remember five hundred and sixty-seven things that you forgot to put on the list.

Once you have completed the tour of your space, it's time to repeat this process, except this time in your virtual and paper space. I typically prefer to go virtual next and scroll through my inbox and desktop, writing down any thoughts or reminders of things that I need or want to do in the next few weeks. Do the same process with papers, although if you're anything like me, the presence of physical papers has gone way down in recent years. Write down any appointments that need to be made, follow-up that needs to happen, or add upcoming events to your calendar.

Finally, you can download the thought download trigger list that I have provided for you on my website. This list is meant to jog your memory and help you feel confident that you have exhausted every item taking up mental energy.

PRO TIP: I first learned this process from David Allen in his book *Getting Things Done*. In this book, Allen recommends a strategy that he calls the two-minute rule. This rule states that if you come across a task that takes less than two minutes to complete, you just do it right then and there instead of adding it to your list. His logic is that by the time you write the task down, organize it, then come back to it and plan a time to do it, you could have already completed the task. Be realistic about the time you have during this thought download session to decide if you want to implement the rule there or not. Because I practice this rule daily, I don't typically use it while I am completing a thought download so that I can get through that process faster. But it is completely up to you and the amount of time that you have left.

I asked Tania to go ahead and complete a thought download before our next session, then we sat together to see what she had come up with. I wasn't surprised when she had over seven pages torn out of her legal pad that she had no idea what to do with next. I typically complete a thought download twice a year, and I find five to eight (overwhelming) pages is about average for me.

A huge part of this process is getting all of these tasks on paper. Once you have done that, however, you need to find a way to take action on these items without being completely paralyzed. This is where your MAP Book comes back into play. I suggest you make three lists in your MAP Book:

- a parking lot for things you would like to do someday
- projects to be done this year
- tasks that will take an hour or less

Now, go through your thought download, and rewrite each item on the appropriate list. You'll be amazed at the continuum of ideas you have written down—from calling your aunt to say hi to redesigning the back-yard. Not all projects are created equally! You may notice as you write down certain tasks that you had gotten caught up in the moment with the thought download, and some of these ideas aren't worthy of making it on any of your lists. That is absolutely okay. But as soon as you rewrite an item on its appropriate list, be sure to cross it off from your original thought download.

By the end of this process, you will have three lists. If you still have some mental energy and time left, this is where I recommend that you prioritize or time rank the ideas on each list. You're obviously not going to get all of these tasks done in a weekend, but by estimating how long each task will take to complete, you increase the chances that it will actually get done. If you notice a certain task that feels really overwhelming, like "Plan Jake's 3rd birthday at BounceTown," then you can break it up into smaller action steps—call BounceTown, buy invitations, write out invitations, send invitations, plan food, order food, buy cake, etc.

If at all possible, decide on the month that you would like to complete the projects and the action items list. Maybe you know that your mother-in-law is taking the kids one Saturday, and you and your partner want to tackle a few things on the list. Or maybe certain projects have completion dates, like your son's birthday party. Whatever you can physically get on your calendar will be a win since you are more likely to complete that task if it is on your calendar.

If you are feeling overwhelmed by this process, you are absolutely not alone, Mama–it's a lot! It definitely doesn't have to happen all at once. I remember the first time that I tried this process. I took a day off of work, and it took the entire day. It's never taken that long since, but the first time is always the most challenging. This is because you are really going back and culling through the archives. If you do this process quarterly, it will hopefully never take that long again.

One question that I get a lot is should my work to-do list items should be included with my family/home life to-do list? I typically separate them myself, but it's completely up to you and what makes the most sense in this season of life.

Now that we have walked through the process let's remember why a thought download is effective. First, you will be amazed at the weight you feel lifted off of your shoulders when these thoughts are written down on paper. There is something purely magical about getting the tasks out of your head and written down somewhere where actual action can be taken on them.

And most importantly, how does this help you reach your goals? Again, you are creating space for them with this thought download system. If you take the time to do this exercise when you are feeling really over- whelmed (likely two to three times a year), you will find that you have more bandwidth. This is because you are no longer carrying every single thing that you need to do in your brain. As a busy mom, this is life-chang- ing and life-giving, I promise!

Strategizing This Quarter:
Quarterly Check-Ins

I truly believe that the biggest misconception that we have as moms is that we need to be doing more. More is not the goal, though, Mama. Just like with time maximization, we want to be investing more of our time in activities that matter and create massive traction toward our goals.

> "I truly believe that the biggest misconception that we have as moms is that we need to doing more. More is not the goal."

That being said, the next strategy for helping you be more productive toward your goals is by doing a quarterly check-in. When I was a teacher, I never thought about the year being divided up into quarters. That wasn't a unit of measure that applied to me at the time. However, once I hit the business world, I quickly realized that everything was about quarter one, quarter two, quarter three, and quarter four. The idea of three-month intervals really intrigued me—just enough time to make real progress but not too much time to get distracted.

This is where quarterly check-ins came in. At the end of each quarter, I set aside an hour or so to do a check-in. My check-in process is painfully simple. In my MAP Book, I write two questions: "What am I proud that I accomplished in the last quarter?" and "What am I looking forward to accomplishing in the next quarter?" I write these questions on the two-facing pages in the back of my MAP Book when I set it up. This is a visual cue to remind me to do this reflection piece.

When I sit down to do this reflection, my first resource is my Google calendar. I look back on the three months and write down anything that I did that I am proud of. Once I have exhausted the calendar, I turn to my annual goals. If I accomplished anything that quarter that moved me closer to those, I include it on this list. For example, each year, I do a Goodreads reading challenge. I try to read about thirty-five books a quarter to keep up with that, so I will add my reading progress to my accomplishment list. Other things that I might add to this list are workout programs that I have completed, money that my business has brought in, or financial goals that our family has hit.

On the next page, it's time to look ahead at the upcoming quarter to think about what I am looking forward to. This exercise really is just priming myself for the upcoming three months and giving me a sneak peek at things to come. First, I consult our family calendar to write down any important events that are coming up. Then, I go through each of my goal areas and decide what has to happen to connect back to having success with my annual goals. Sometimes, this is a financial goal, a health goal, a reading goal, or a personal growth activity goal.

Taking the time to do a quarterly reflection is beneficial for a number of reasons. First, it forces me to hit the pause button and celebrate how much happened in the last three months. Despite the number of times I've done this exercise, I am still in awe over how much actually gets accomplished in three months. It's always more than I expect. Second, it helps me genuinely start to get excited about the next three months. A three-month stretch usually pushes us into another season, so it prepares me mentally for things to come (I'm looking at you, winter). Finally, a quarterly check-in forces me to be proactive. I begin to think about upcoming goals and events, strategizing about next steps and supports that may need to be put in place. I typically leave my quarterly reflection feeling energized and ready to tackle anything, knowing that I have identified the most important goals that need my attention.

Getting Consistent: Weekly Check-Ins

If a quarterly check-in feels overwhelming for you right now, consider starting with a weekly check-in. This process is especially effective if you are hoping to build up the habit of reflection and being strategic with your time.

In Michael Hyatt's book, *Free to Focus*, he shares a weekly review process in Chapter Eight that he uses that I appreciate the simplicity of. Each week, he asks himself: "What big wins did I have this week?" and "What didn't work this week?" in terms of your goals and priorities.

By asking yourself these questions regularly, you are forcing yourself to acknowledge when you are prioritizing your goals and when you are not. A lot of moms shy away from holding up this mirror. But, Mama, there is no shame in this. If you were working on running your first 5K, then your kiddo got a whopping ear infection that derailed your plans. There is nothing wrong with that. You just simply did not make the progress you expected to make.

This information will help you to plan for your next week to help you prioritize going forward. In order to be a proactive mom, you need to be constantly reflecting on your goals and on the progress of your goals in an open and honest way.

Purposefully Bringing It All Together: How to Plan Your Year

January is my favorite month of the year. I mean, don't get me wrong, I really dislike the bitter cold in New England. But I love, love, love taking the whole month to plan the year ahead. There's just something so motivating and inspiring about having a whole twelve-month stretch ahead of you to dream up whatever you want to do!

This may be an unpopular opinion, but I give myself the entire month of January to reflect, create, and strategize goals for the year ahead. I used to rush to try to make all of my goals come together in the week after Christmas. That changed after kids, though, when it feels like a bomb went off in your house, and you're so exhausted from December that you can barely string together a coherent thought.

So, Mama, give yourself permission to take all the time that you need to set meaningful goals that will actually help you move toward your dream life vision. Gone are the days of picking an arbitrary goal just so you don't feel like a slacker on New Year's Eve. No more "I'm going to lose ten pounds this year!" or "I'm going to yell at my kids less." None of those are going to move you toward your dream life vision, so we need to dig deeper than that. Let's do this!

Step 1: Conducting an Annual Review

My first step when planning for the year ahead is to do an annual review. An annual review is the time I set aside in December to reflect on the previous year. I do a four-step process, broken up over the course of the month.

My annual review looks like:
- Using my time tracker for a week (see Chapter Five)
- Complete a calendar reflection:
  - What did I enjoy doing this year?
  - What did I not enjoy doing this year?
  - What do I want to say yes to in the future?
  - What do I want to say no to in the future?
- Brainstorm answers to my favorite personal reflection questions:
  - What did I accomplish this year?
  - What went well this year?
  - What do I want to challenge myself with?

- What habits did I establish this year?
- What habits do I want to give up in the new year?
  What habits do I want to start in the new year?
- What do I want more of in the coming year?
- Complete a business review

If you want to see the full process of how I complete my annual review, you will find a resource on my website to walk you through each step.

The annual review is important because it helps you examine where you are coming from. Was last year awesome? Perfect, your momentum is high. Let's keep this party going. Was last year a dumpster fire? Okie dokie, you may need to give yourself some grace and some extra time on the runway. Be sure not to skip this reflection step when you are getting ready to set goals for the upcoming year.

Step 2: Vision of My Life in 365 Days

While I don't generally take a lot of time to do visualization exercises, I do generally enjoy pondering the question: what do I want my life to look like on December 31st of next year? Three hundred sixty-five days from now, who do I want to be? What do I want to have accomplished? For me, this is the perfect prompt because a year doesn't feel so long that you can't imagine it. At the same time, it's not so short that you feel as though there isn't time to get anything done.

Let's do this exercise together now. Take out your MAP Book and write at the top, "Where I want to be on December 31st of 20XX." Set a timer for fifteen minutes and do a thought download. Allow yourself to dream. What would you like to accomplish, experience, celebrate?

Here is my list: by the end of this year, I would like to:
- Have held my published book in my hands.
- Had my first six-figure year, ever.

- Go on a winter retreat to somewhere warm.
- Relaxing vacation in Maine with the family.
- Be 50% of the way toward our financial goal of a down payment for lake house.
- Hire an assistant in my photography business.
- Complete two hundred rides on the Peloton.

Even just writing these things out gets me excited for the new year! Now, it's important that you don't stop the process here. These aren't goals. They are the end results of the goals that you set. This is just the dream stage, where you begin to see what's possible. We'll get into setting actual yearly goals in the next step.

Step 3: Create Your Yearly Goals

Finally, it's time to turn these goals into plans! Are you beginning to see why it takes me the entire month of January to do this process?

At this point, I take my end-of-year dream list and begin to turn the end results into action steps. What do I need to do to make sure that I am holding a published book in my hand by December 31st? Well, I need to write the dang book. Okay, how am I going to do that? I am going to wake up an hour before my kids every day and write at least one thousand words a day. Boom. That's the goal.

Let's break down another goal for the sake of the example. One of our financial goals this year is to save up 50% of a down payment for our future lake house. We're estimating 50% to be about $40,000–that's a decent amount of money! Now it's time to brainstorm...what could I do to make sure that we are bringing home an extra $40,000? Well, my husband is a teacher, so it's unlikely he'll be getting a $40,000 bonus this year. That means I will have to plan to make that happen with my business. I will need to create some new income streams to bring in some additional cash flow. This will turn into the goal: I will make $40,000 in passive income this year. I can break it down further later, but for right now, I'd say that is a pretty lofty goal!

Speaking of lofty goals, don't be afraid to go big here. I am a big believer in putting what you want out into the universe. It's only January. Aim high and adjust later.

After you have created your personal goals for the entire year, you can begin to break those down into quarterly goals. What's a quarterly goal? It's a goal that takes about three months to accomplish. You definitely don't want to have too many of these. I generally have between one and two for my personal life. Then, I have separate goals for my family and my business that are quarterly.

Step 4: Create Family Goals

The next step in this process is to create family goals. I have done this several different ways over the years. When my kids were young, my husband and I would do this process together. We would think of twelve things we wanted to do over the course of the year–experiences we wanted our kids to have and skills we wanted to develop. We would post these goals on our refrigerator. Then, every time we found ourselves with "What should we do this weekend?" we would have a great starting point.

As our kids got older, our goal process evolved to include them. In 2022, we decided that we wanted to explore different passions as a family. We assigned each month a passion area–such as animals, woodworking, learning Spanish, bird watching, and martial arts. Then, we spent time each month exploring those areas.

Even if you only set one goal for your family for the entire year, you are still walking your family through the goal-setting process. I highly recommend having a family meeting when your kids are old enough to start thinking about what you want to experience as a family this year.

Step 5: Create Personal Goals

Now, you may be wondering how personal goals are different from your yearly goals. The truth is, they are not terribly different. For me, though, there are a few goals that I set every year that I have running in the background. Keep in mind that I have been doing this goal-setting process for almost ten years now, so you may not be quite ready for this if you are new to annual goal-setting.

When I set personal goals for the year, they typically revolve around the number of books I want to read, workouts that I want to tackle, and habits that I want to adopt.

Here are some examples:
- Book Challenge: Read 150 books this year.
- Workouts: Complete 200 Peloton rides.
- Habits: Write 1,000 words a day; wake up at 5:00 AM daily.

Whatever goals you decide to set, make sure they are actionable. You should be able to look at your goal list and know whether or not you have achieved your goal. If you're not sure, make it more specific. For example, if your goal is "Feel confident in my skin," decide what that means. I would encourage you to attach that to an action, like "I will work out Monday through Friday for thirty minutes a day." When you look at that goal at the end of the year, you will confidently be able to say that you did it or didn't do it. Finally, make sure your goals excite you. If they don't, go back to the drawing board. Dream bigger. Think about December of next year—what would make it the best year yet? Push yourself! And remember, you can always reach out if you need support creating goals that light you up!

Kicking It Up a Notch:
Going from 12-Month to 12-Week Goals

During the 2020 COVID pandemic, I had a chance to pull out a book that had been sitting untouched on my shelf for months, entitled The 12 Week Year by Brian Moran and Michael Lennington. The premise of this book is that instead of creating goals at the beginning of the year that you lose momentum with, break one single year up into four smaller "years," if you will. I was definitely intrigued by this idea, especially because during the lockdown, I wasn't really able to predict what was coming next.

To give my days a little more structure, I decided to give the twelve-week year a try, and it was pivotal in my ability to accomplish some big goals during that tumultuous time. According to the authors Moran and Lenngington, the twelve-week year capitalizes on the fact that we have so much more motivation when the finish line is in sight. In January, it is so easy to set goals that are long forgotten by the time summer rolls around. So, instead of setting goals for a twelve-month stretch, you set smaller goals for a smaller length of time. He suggests twelve weeks, with a buffer of one week, to recalibrate and prepare for the next twelve-week sprint.

By setting your goals in this way, you are also providing your future self with flexibility and the ability to pivot if another goal or opportunity arises. During the pandemic, it was impossible for me to predict what I would be doing in twelve months or what the world would look like. I had been wearing the same yoga pants for two weeks at that point (maybe a bit of an exaggeration...but not much!). Action had to be planned and implemented quickly to stick with the timetable, and I was super motivated to make it happen.

When I sat down to map out my twelve-week year, the first thing I did was to decide on one goal to focus on. That goal was to have a completed book proposal that was ready to be shared with a publisher at the end of the twelve weeks. I did a little bit of research and found a book that would walk me through the book proposal project since this was all brand new to me. This book really helped me to plan my action steps for each week since each chapter was broken down into tangible steps. I adapted the steps so that they fit within the twelve-week time frame, grouping two activities together if they looked like they could easily be accomplished within a week.

I created a chart in my MAP Book to track each week with the activity that I had to do. As I went, I changed the action steps as needed. But the action steps, along with the tight time frame, kept me chugging along every morning. I was focused on what had to happen, and at the end of twelve weeks, I had a completed book proposal in my hands.

This goal-setting strategy was addicting, and once I had my first successful run, I went for another. This time, my business was back up and running, so I used it to plan for profit in my photography business. After that quarter was achieved, I used it to start creating the website for my coaching business.

I tend to set goals around my businesses, but my coaching clients have also used this twelve-week year to set goals that they want to take immediate, intense action on. One of my clients had a goal of having her daughter's nursery set up by the time she went out on maternity leave. We used the twelve-week year to babystep her plan and make sure that it happened. Another client decided to use the twelve-week year to get consistent with her workout routines. She was so motivated by the twelve-week year that the next quarter, she actually pursued two goals at the same time!

If you are looking for a way to take action quickly on your goals, the twelve-week year might be the right fit for you.

12 Week Year Goal Template

12 Week Goals

Goal #1:
Goal #2:

Goal #1:

Consistent Action	Due

How To Set Goals When You Are Overwhelmed

If you are reading this chapter during a season of life while things are slow, you may feel fired up right now. It is important to acknowledge, though, that there will be a season where you are overwhelmed, stressed, and do not give a hoot about your goals because there is a raging dumpster fire in front of you that you need to deal with, pronto.

So, to conclude this chapter, here is a word of advice. When you feel overwhelmed, give yourself grace. Take a week off from your goals. Don't take two weeks off from your goals. But acknowledge the season of life, acknowledge the burnout, and put a date on your calendar to revisit what you are working toward.

We all hit a time when our systems fall apart, our habits fly out the window, and the last things we can think about are our long-term goals. That doesn't mean that they aren't important. It just means they can't have our full attention right now.

LET'S MAKE A PLAN!

- Complete a thought download in one setting that is stressing you out the most (work, home, etc.). Use your MAP Book to organize your list so nothing falls through the cracks.
- Decide if quarterly or weekly check-ins could work to help you get more strategic and consistent.
- Create a plan to either utilize twelve-month or twelve-week goals to make progress faster.

Up Next

In Chapter Eight, you will:

- Identify positive habits that you currently have and/ or would like to have.
- Learn about five strategies that will help you stay accountable to your positive habits (they are the building blocks of your dream life, after all!).
- Be inspired to create systems to become more efficient across all areas of your life so that you can spend more of your time working toward your dream life.

CHAPTER EIGHT

Establishing Positive Daily Habits

One of my very first clients, Vanessa, came to me when she was feeling at an all-time low. All of the things that she thought she had wanted–to be a stay-at-home mom, to leave her career, to make her own schedule–had happened. On paper, she was living her "dream life."

And yet, she was struggling. She had gotten to the point where she was questioning if she should have had children if she should have married her husband, and if she would ever be confident in her skin again. Vanessa shared that her anxiety about these things was getting so bad that she seldom left the house with her children because the thought just overwhelmed her, and it was easier to stay home. She was doing things she never thought she would do, like giving her young kids unlimited screen time so she could scroll on social media. These are big, valid concerns and ones that are shared by so many moms. The fact that Vanessa had identified her struggles and gotten proactive with them is so amazing.

Obviously, there was a lot to tackle here. As a first step, I asked Vanessa to walk me through her routine every day. She was making the necessities of her daily life happen, but nothing more than that. Every morning, her husband would wake up really early to go to work. She would then sleep until her son and daughter woke up, around 8:00 AM. At that point, it was all about entertaining them, feeding them, and making sure everyone stayed in one piece until her husband returned home around dinner time. They would eat together, watch TV until midnight, and then go to bed to do it all over again the next day.

It was clear from this conversation that Vanessa's habits weren't serving her. Despite the fact that she was a stay-at-home mom, it didn't sound like she had a lot of routines or consistency in her day. When I asked what she did for fun, Vanessa told me that her favorite thing to do was to read…but she hadn't read a book since her oldest had been born four years earlier.

Together, Vanessa and I started the hard work of tackling her habits in priority order. This can be a really overwhelming process, so it is extremely helpful to tackle this process with another person who can help you see your blind spots. Before we go too far into Vanessa's next steps, let's take a moment to calibrate our definition of the word "habit."

Identifying Positive Habits

You can't open a personal growth book or turn on a personal growth podcast without hearing the word "habit." Habits are specific actions that are triggered by a certain event. For example, when you get in your car, you may immediately put on your seatbelt. Why? Because it's a habit. The action that triggers it is sitting in the seat and closing the door. Putting on the actual seat belt is a habit.

When you stop to think about it, most of what we do as humans is habitual. This is (usually) a good thing. What a lot of people don't realize, though, is you have the ability to harness your habits and utilize them to make positive changes in your life.

Right now, open up your MAP Book and write a list of any current habits that you have. Start at the time that you wake up in the morning and go until bedtime.

Here are some ideas to get you started:
- Brush teeth
- Let dogs out
- Eat breakfast
- Check lunch calendar
- Take vitamin
- Workout
- Coffee date with husband
- Write for thirty minutes
- Take shower
- Hugging and kissing the kids before they got on the bus
- Listen to audiobook on the way to work
- Guided meditation before starting the workday
- Sun lamp on while responding to emails
- Walk at lunchtime

Once you have identified all of your current habits, go ahead and label them with a plus sign (+) for a positive habit that is contributing to your life and a dash (-) for a negative habit that is not necessarily moving you forward. Then, draw a dot next to any habit that is a neutral habit—it's not necessarily helping you or negatively affecting you. It just happens (for example: listening to music on your commute to work).

Now, on the same page, write down any habits that you WISHED you had. Here are some ideas to get you started:

- Working out for thirty minutes a day

- Reading ten pages a day
- Going outside for ten minutes
- Calling a friend or a loved one
- Inbox Zero
- Not scrolling mindlessly on your phone
- Flossing
- Waking up early
- Meditation
- Yoga/stretching

At the moment, the list of habits you desire may feel daunting. If that's the case, you're not alone! That's a completely normal, natural part of the process. We're going to narrow down your focus to think about just the habits that will impact your life the most right now.

Look back at this list and ask yourself: What is the one habit that will change everything for me? Be honest here (for me, it was waking up early. I didn't want to do it. Heck, I still don't want to do it every day at 5:01 AM when my alarm goes off. But I knew that would be my game changer).

Vanessa knew that the habit that would change everything was moving her body. At the time, she wasn't doing anything to lose the forty pounds she was so stressed about. The stress was causing her to eat more than she knew she should, and the scale was going in the wrong direction. She knew if she started regularly moving her body, things would start to fall into place. So that was where we decided to start our work on her habits.

Even by narrowing our focus on this one habit, Vanessa still felt overwhelmed. She was nervous that she wouldn't be able to stick with it and would wind up being disappointed in herself again. With the right coaching and the right accountability system, though, implementing new habits won't be as challenging as you think!

Accountability: Tracking Your Habits

Once you have identified the one habit that will have the biggest impact, it's time to come up with a system for tracking your habits and holding yourself accountable.

Visually Track Your Streaks
The first strategy that I suggest if you are hoping to get consistent with a new habit is the most simple of them all: using sticky notes to track your streaks. When I was trying to get consistent with my workouts, I posted a sticky note in the doorway of our kitchen each time I completed a thirty-minute workout. I "celebrated" my consistent progress toward this habit with the sticky note. The challenge was that if I skipped a day, I had to take down all of the sticky notes and start over. I distinctly remember lying in bed a few mornings, not wanting to work out. Then, the thought of having my daughters watch me take down all of the sticky notes that I had been collecting motivated me to get out of bed and get moving.

Why does this strategy work? For me, it worked for a few reasons. First, I am super visual. I need to see the progress being tracked in some way. Second, I am super competitive—especially with myself. And finally, this accountability felt "public." House guests would walk into our kitchen and immediately ask what the sticky notes were. In addition, my kids would make observations about how long my streak was, and then we would all be super sad if I had to take them down to start over. Will this definitely work for you? No, not definitely. But if you are a visual person, too, who wants to compete with yourself to challenge yourself to the next level, it's worth a try. At the end of the day, all you will be out is a few sticky notes!

One final note about the sticky note strategy is that you may want to override the urge to do something "just five times a week." Especially with something like working out, it is best to get started with daily implementation. When I was focusing on daily workouts, that meant that I would do a thirty-minute Hiit workout five times a week and then make sure that I did something that I considered an active recovery workout the other two days. It wasn't just about the workout. It was about the consistency of the habit.

Habit Tracker

The second strategy that I suggest for getting consistent with a new habit is to create a habit tracker. I was first introduced to this idea in Darren Hardy's book, The Compound Effect, where he shares his tracker. You can see a sample of what this could look like below. On the left side, I wrote down all of the habits that I wanted to include in my life for which I wanted to track my progress. I decided how many times a week I wanted that habit to happen. Just like I mentioned with the sticky note tracker, though, be careful with deciding if you only want a habit to happen a couple of times a week. In my experience and in the experiences my clients have shared with me, I have found that new habits are easier to get consistent when implemented daily, at least in the beginning.

Weekly Rhythm Register: Week of _____

"The rhythm of daily action aligned with your goals creates the momentum that separates the dreamers from the super-achievers." — Darren Hardy

CONSISTENCY OVER INTENSITY

HABIT	M	T	W	Th	F	Sa	Su	Achieved	Goal	Net
4am Wake-up									7	
Photography Hustle									5	
Three Water Bottles									7	
Coffee Date									5	
Daily Exercize (30 min.)									4	
Sun lamp/time outside									5	
Floss									7	
Yoga/meditation (10 min.)									6	
Daily Planning									7	
9:30 Lights out									5	
No Sugar									7	
Totals									65	

I love numbers, so being able to add up my totals each day and then see how close I made it to my goal for the week was very motivating for me. I would try to really focus on one goal each week, and then anything else that also happened was a bonus. I could also use the week before to set goals for the upcoming week, meaning I was encouraging at least 1% growth every week. That growth adds up, Mama!

Tracking Habits in Your MAP Book

If you recently got started using your MAP Book, I would highly recommend that you use your notebook to track your progress toward your habits. I have five habits that I try to hit every single day—wake up at 5:00 AM, work out, write five things I'm grateful for, drink 120 oz of water, and eat a salad.

In my notebook every day, I write the numbers 1-5 in the upper right-hand corner. As I complete a habit, I cross off the number then circle the final number that I achieved that day. It's a super easy way to track my progress in less than thirty seconds a day. However, if you're finding this isn't motivating enough for you, you may want to try to start with the habit tracker shared previously in this chapter or add an accountability group for added motivation (more about accountability groups in a moment!)

October 3rd   1
                                     2
My affirmations   3
· I am a present mom.   4
· I am an exceptional wife.   5
· I am in the best shape of my life.

Goal Activities:

· Girl dates
· Date night
· Liift 4

Priority Tasks:

· mini golf with daughter
· marketing presentation
· Workout, Day 2

Gratitudes:

· A husband that makes me the perfect
  coffee every morning
· Being able to do my workouts in
  my living room
· Having a flexible schedule
· So motivated by yesterday's
  podcast episode
· A dry bed on a rainy day

Tasks:

· Call Mom
· make vet appt. for Lucy

There's An App For That

With modern technology, there are so many apps that can help you track your habits. I tend to be old school, so sticky notes and handwritten charts in my MAP Book are more my jam. There's something about writing the habits down that just empowers me.

With that being said, I have also found great success with websites and apps that help you track your progress in a variety of areas: nutrition, reading, workouts, water intake, etc. A great example of this is Goodreads.

At the beginning of the year, I set a goal for the number of books that I want to read—this drives my daily reading habit. For this year, my goal was to read 150 books in 365 days, which works out to be about three books a week (one audiobook, one fiction, one nonfiction book). By using Goodreads, they track the number of books that I'm reading when I provide a quick update, and it serves as a great visual representation of my reading life. I occasionally get emails that update me on how I'm progressing on my reading challenge, and I can see the challenges of my friends for extra motivation.

So, if you are looking for a way to hold yourself accountable, it could be worth it to see if there is a website or app that could help provide you with positive reinforcement.

Accountability Group
Finally, the last strategy to hold yourself accountable for getting consistent with your habits is to form an accountability group or create an accountability partnership. A lot of my coaching clients shy away from this option because they don't think anyone in their lives is on a similar journey. You would be surprised!

If you're just getting started with a new habit, an accountability partner would be ideal. When I first decided that I wanted to be the healthiest version of myself possible, my husband agreed to help me stay accountable. In the beginning, he actually did the workouts with me, and we worked together to adjust our portion sizes and grocery shopping trips. After a little while, though, he went back to his routines, and I just shared with him every morning how my workout went. So, your accountability partner doesn't have to be someone who is following your journey exactly. You also may be surprised at who else is quietly on their journey and wants accountability as much as you do.

Every year in October, I do the Last 90 Days challenge. This was first introduced to me by Rachel Hollis in 2018. The idea is that you gain momentum in the last three months of the year so that you go into the new year strong rather than starting at zero. I knew I wanted to do this, but with the holidays, I knew it would be a struggle. I put out on my Facebook page that I was going to give this challenge a try and asked if any ladies wanted to join me.

The expectation was that every day at 8:00 PM, we would send a group message with the number of habits we completed that day. No explanation necessary! Just a way to hold yourself accountable. I can't tell you how many days I got out of bed just because I wanted to hit my goal to share with the group that night. The accountability group took less than three minutes a day to participate in and helped me make way more growth than I would have made on my own.

Implementing High-Leverage Systems

John Maxwell and James Clear inspired a lot of my work with designing systems. As I dug deeper into designing systems that brought me closer to my dream life, I realized that systems were actually more effective for me than setting goals. Wait, what? Hold the phone! Did the personal growth coach just say systems are better than GOALS? Yep, sure did.

In John Maxwell's book, *15 Invaluable Laws of Growth*, he defines a system as "a process for predictably achieving a goal, based on specific, orderly, repeatable principles and practices. Systems are deliberate, intentional, and practical." I couldn't have said it better myself. In busy mom terms, a system is repeatable actions that will achieve a specific outcome.

I can honestly say that I live on systems. And I definitely thrive on systems. I have systems for working out, for taking notes, for organizing my life (hello, MAP Book, you're so pretty), for grocery shopping, and for cleaning.

> "You do not rise to the level of goals, you fall to the level of your systems."
>
> – James Clear

In *Atomic Habits*, author James Clear reminds us of the difference between goals and systems. A goal, according to Clear, is about achievable results. But a system is about a process that leads to results.

Let's take cleaning as an example. A cleaning goal would be "I want a clean house once a week." A system would be "I am going to tackle one ten-minute cleaning task a day to ensure I have a clean house each week." See the difference? One is a process; one is "you either did, or you didn't."

The cool thing about systems is that once you set it, you can forget it. I established my cleaning system a year ago. On Mondays, I dust; on Tuesdays, I vacuum, etc., etc. Now, I don't even have to put it on my daily to-do list because it is just what I do. I don't have to think about it, and it's super easy to delegate. If I can't do it on Monday morning while my daughters eat breakfast, I ask my husband if he can do it after work.

My favorite quote from *Atomic Habits* is, "You do not rise to the level of goals, you fall to the level of your systems." It is so true!

Imagine you are just starting on your dream life journey and decide you need a system for working out. Your goal is to lose twenty-five pounds, but you keep starting and stopping, trying different things, and aren't hitting your goal. Most people get frustrated here. But what they don't realize: it's not the goal's fault. You need a system to get to the goal.

So, what could your system be? For me, my working out system is to pick an at-home program (I use BeachBody on Demand, as does my husband) that usually lasts about eight weeks. My system is to complete the workout at 5:00 AM every morning and do at least seven thousand steps a day. On rest days, I walk ten thousand steps and do yoga. That's my system. There's no thinking other than deciding on the program and setting my alarm.

Some of my other basic systems include my MAP Book (which you know about), marriage check-ins, morning routine, budgeting, and cleaning.

Of course, you know me at this point. I have some more complex systems as well, such as how I plan my weeks and lay out my daily plans. But I decided once, and now I depend on the system. In the rest of this chapter, we will explore how to establish and implement your own systems for success.

Creating Your Own Systems

So, how can you create a system for yourself? First, try to choose the one habit that you know you need a system for or the key habit that will make the biggest impact on your goals.

Have you picked something? Awesome. Now, this is the challenging part: what matters most about your system? What is the most simple way to accomplish it?

Let's say you chose budgeting. You may have to do some foundational work to set yourself up, like creating a budget with your partner, maybe tracking some spending. But after that is done, what is your system for checking in on the budget? Are you going to log on every day and update a spreadsheet? Are you going to have a budget meeting once a week with your partner? Are you going to calibrate your budget daily, weekly, monthly? It seems overwhelming to make all these decisions, but re-member, you only have to do so once.

Once these decisions are made, it's time to implement your system. You need to make your system super visible so that you have a constant reminder of what you are trying to establish. When I am establishing a system, I write the system's action step in my Big Three on my daily MAP Book page every day. So, if I was establishing a budgeting system, I would write "Check on budget" (ten minutes) on my daily to-do list. I would do this every day (or every week) until it became automatic. I did that for our cleaning routine, and now, if the kids are eating breakfast, I just need to remember what day it is to know what task I'm doing. Keep it simple, and before you know it, you'll be basking in the glow of a productive system that is getting you to your goals faster.

Are you starting to see why I am way more obsessed with systems than goals?! Let's explore one of my favorite habits, which I turned into a sys-tem to help me create my dream life while my husband and kids were sleeping!

My Morning System
My favorite system? Waking up at 5:00 AM. Okay, hold on, hold on—don't turn the page yet. Let me preface by saying that I HATE waking up at 5:00 AM. I loathe it. Setting that alarm guts me every time. But it's the system that gives me the most benefits, so hear me out!

Here is the system, which, believe it or not, starts the night before:
- My "go to bed" alarm goes off at 8:55 PM each night. This reminds me that I need to get my act together (which usually involves rolling off the couch) and get to bed.
- Before I go upstairs, I roll out my yoga mat and set up my workout program for the following morning. I will also put my MAP Book on the couch.

- Off to bed I go!
- At 5:01 AM, my alarm goes off. It is set to not be snooze-able. That is completely on purpose! In order for the system to work, it needs to be consistent.
- I get downstairs and hit "play" on my workout. There's no thinking that happens before this. Get downstairs, tie shoes, hit play. That is a part of the system design. Sometimes, I "wake up" halfway through the workout!
- When the workout is done, I set up my notebook page for the day until my husband comes in for our coffee date. We hang out until 6:30 AM, and then I write for thirty minutes or do my personal growth work while he gets ready for his day.
- My kiddos need to be up around 7:00 AM to make it to the bus on time, so just like that, my day officially begins!

Staying Accountable

Now, as I mentioned, I do not like waking up early. That being said, I get a rush when I know that I have completed my most important tasks for the day before breakfast and then have the whole day ahead to tackle everything else.

But in order for this system to happen, I needed to make the early wake-up a habit. How did I do this? In a few different ways:

- When I first started trying this, I would plan to wake up to do an activity that I was excited about or that I wouldn't have time for otherwise. For me, it was my photography class. I was super motivated. Maybe you don't ever get to read, or journal, or paint, or do yoga. Promise yourself time to do those things when you get up with the alarm. If you start with waking up to work out or to do another activity you aren't excited about, you may lose momentum quickly.

- As I mentioned before, I set the alarm on my phone so that it wasn't able to be snoozed. I also labeled the alarm with the activity that I was excited to wake up and do (example: Photography Class!) as a reminder for the morning.
- I implemented the sticky note system at first so that I could visually see how many days in a row I succeeded in my habit. And yes, I even woke up early on weekends in the beginning!
- For a while, I would send a message to my accountability group to say good morning. Somehow, knowing the time stamp was on there was super motivating!
- Eventually, I moved to my habit tracker, where I still record my early wake-ups to this day.

When you are getting started with a system, do not be afraid to share it with others. Not only will this keep you accountable, but it also might help you to motivate others (and yourself) at the same time!

How Systems Will Change Your Life

Remember Vanessa from the beginning of this chapter? As Vanessa began to hone in on the habits that were going to serve her best, she slowly began to develop systems. When we met recently, our conversation centered around how these systems were becoming automated and really providing her with the bandwidth to think about other things.

Here are some of my favorite benefits of using systems on your personal growth journey:

Decide Once
First, systems allow you to decide once. You no longer have to exert mental and emotional energy, wondering if you should do something,

how you should do it, when you should do it. Nope, nope! Systems free you from all that and allow you to get right to it.

For example, you can decide that you work out every weekday morning at 6:00 AM. There, it is decided! You no longer have to spend time figuring out when your workout is going to happen. It sounds like such a small thing, but once you start deciding once for what to wear, what to eat, how you shut down your workday, etc., you will be liberated.

Remove the Emotion
Systems also allow you to remove your emotions. The best example of this is morning workouts. When I worked out in the afternoon after work, I would spend my entire day concocting reasons why I did not have to work out. I would then pitch those excuses to my husband when I arrived home. One day, he (lovingly) told me that it didn't really affect him if I worked out or not. Oof, that was a reality check.

By moving my workouts to the morning, I did not spend all day thinking about why I did not want to do it. The system kicked in, and I just did it on autopilot.

The Compound Effect
Again, if you want to be really motivated about the idea of habits and compounding results, I highly recommend that you get your hands on Darren Hardy's book, *The Compound Effect*. The premise of the book is that small steps add up. The book illustrates this concept in so many profound ways. And once you put it into practice and see that it is true? You will be just as enthusiastic about systems as I am!

Consistency > Intensity
I loved this concept so much that I have it written on the top of my habit tracker so that I read it every day: consistency > intensity. The idea is that it is way more important to be consistent than to be intense. You can

only mentally prepare to do something intense once in a while. But if you take intensity off the table, it is way easier to just be consistent.

Again, working out is a great example of this. Some mornings, my alarm would go off, and I would think to myself, "This is not going to happen today. I am (fill in the blank: tired, sick, sore, etc.)." I would tell myself, "Okay, you don't have to do the workout. You just have to watch it." Another one I would use is "Just do the warm-up and then watch the rest." That would seem doable in my pre-caffeinated brain, so I would get downstairs, turn on the workout, and before I knew it, I was repping with the rest of them.

It didn't have to be my best workout; I didn't need to beat any personal records, but it happened. And guess what? It is way more likely to happen again tomorrow because I did it today. Spoiler alert: I have been consistently working out for six years now, and I have never once just done the warm-up or watched the workout. If it works, it works!

I want to take a second to add a disclaimer here as we wrap up this section about habits and system creation: acknowledge your season of life, Mama. If you have a newborn that's up every two hours, you are not doing this right now. Save this chapter for a year from now when you might be able to safely put it into practice. Kick yourself in the pants if you're making excuses, but if you are in a season of life where rest is best, you do you, Mama.

LET'S MAKE A PLAN!

- Create a list of positive habits that you currently have or would like to have.
- Choose a strategy that you believe will help you stay accountable for adopting these habits.
- Make a list of systems that you would like to implement that will help you to spend more time on things that matter most.

Up Next

In Chapter Nine, you will:

- Learn four strategies to help you identify your passions as a busy mom.
- Explore some common mom struggles (and their solutions!) when it comes to making time for your own pursuits.

CHAPTER NINE

Finding
Your Passions

The first time I ran a six-week group coaching program, I was shocked that the topic moms wanted to discuss the most was how to find your passion. Why was it that so many moms were feeling as though they didn't know what they were passionate about in their thirties and forties?

Taylor, one of the moms in the group, shared that she had always been passionate about becoming and being a mom. Other moms in the group nodded in agreement. All of her energy, finances, and time went into creating the dream life she decided on in high school: graduate from college, get married, buy a house, have babies. A day came when she realized she had done all that and suddenly felt like she had lost direction. What was she supposed to do now, now that she was living the life she once dreamed of?

All of the moms in the group made it super clear that they weren't unhappy with the way their life plans unfolded. Like mine, the eighteen-year-old vision of their future selves sort of dropped off after those big life events happened. After all, what eighteen-year-old can envision what life is like with a three-year-old and a five-year-old?

If you are like the moms in this group coaching program, you know that now really isn't the time to start a sky-diving hobby or go backpacking through Europe. That being said, we need to make space for ourselves to rekindle passions and find new ones. The goal of identifying your passions is not to add another thing to your endless to-do list. In the group coaching session, that was super clear. You aren't finding a passion so that you can start a new side hustle or leave your job or any of that. Finding your passion is simply that: discovering an activity or an idea that inspires you, allows you to use your creativity, and emphasizes your own individuality within your family unit.

Finding My Passions: The Happiness Project

Fairly early in my personal growth journey, I discovered Gretchen Rubin. She wrote the book *The Happiness Project*, and I was immediately intrigued by the title. I absolutely never buy books unless they are ones that I know I will re-read again and again, and after I borrowed his book from the library, I quickly ordered it on Amazon. Yes, it's that good!

In the book, Rubin shared a similar sentiment that the group coaching moms shared. She was a mom of two girls, in a happy marriage with a job she was satisfied with, yet she somehow felt incomplete. Time was slipping by faster than she was comfortable with, and she wanted to dedicate some time as a journalist to explore science-based research and age-old wisdom about how to be happier in her daily life.

Rubin labeled this experiment "The Happiness Project," in which she walks the reader through her process of dedicating each month to a different area to focus her energy on and action steps. For example, in January, she focused on boosting her energy. The action steps that she had for January included: going to sleep earlier, exercising better, decluttering, tackling a nagging task, and acting more energetic.

After reading this book, I was so inspired to create my own happiness project. This actually prompted my very first personal growth plan. Right now, pause to think about how you could create a happiness project in your life. If you had to focus each month on a different area of your life, what would your top twelve be? What strategies would you want to experiment with? It's a fun idea to think about and definitely, an inspiring read as you begin to think about what your dream life action plan might look like.

Before we dive into how to identify your passions now, as a busy mom, take a moment to set up a page or two for your passion work in your MAP Book. These exercises are going to lead you through a few different passion areas, and having a compiled list is going to be beneficial for you when you go to create your three-year action plan.

Identifying Your Passions

As a child, I distinctly remember knowing all of my classmate's passions: Melanie loved frogs, Chris was passionate about acting, Amanda loved fashion, and Anna was obsessed with reading. I distinctly remember having this realization one day, immediately followed by a veil of despair: what was I passionate about?

At the time, I decided that I didn't have any passions. I wasn't "good" at anything, which I realized as an adult was because of my fixed mindset. Looking back, I realize that I felt there was no way for me to acquire a skill if I wasn't born with it. I truly believed everyone was born a soccer star or a math whiz. It didn't occur to me that everyone has to start somewhere. It felt too "late" for me to learn any of these things, so I just conceded to the idea that I had no passions.

Now that I have a better grasp on the idea of a growth mindset, it's easy to look back and realize that I did have passions as a child. I truly loved working with kids and teaching others new things. Passions of mine also included reading, writing, and planning. Of course, as a kid, these passion areas didn't make me super popular. But I was an introvert, and I remember getting truly giddy about the idea of a new notebook or wandering a library.

When I think back on these passions, my whole life trajectory clicks into focus. Ah, yes. Those passions are the reason I joined the Education Club (met my husband), became a teacher, became a photographer, and then became a dream life designer for busy moms. It all makes sense in hindsight. Basically, I needed to come full circle to realize that my passions from childhood are still things that I feel strongly about now.

If you think about it, what I really did was take my passions and create a job that didn't exist back when I was in fifth grade. Can you imagine going back to tell eleven-year-old Sharon that she's a personal growth coach for busy moms who writes blog posts (writing), creates courses (education), and gets to read personal growth books (reading) as part of her job? I think her mind would be blown because who knew thirty years ago that this could even be a thing? Not me!

As you begin to think about your passions as a child, don't dismiss any of them. I love creating a list for this in my MAP Book so that I can come back to it to reflect on later. As a child, what did you truly get excited about? Was it watching movies or video games? Was it flying a kite with your grandfather? Was it baking cupcakes at your aunt's house? I can still conjure that excited feeling in my stomach when I would get a surge of excitement over something I was passionate about. Can you feel that too?

If you have not already, dedicate a page in your current MAP Book to passion lists. The first one is "Things I Was Passionate About as a Child/Teenager." Then, write down everything that pops into your head, even if it feels random or irrelevant now.

As you begin to add other lists on this page, you may see connections form that you would not see if these were not written down. This may be a practice you want to carry to future MAP Books to serve as a constant reminder of what lights you up.

Wander A Library Or A Bookstore

Once you have created your list of passions you were truly excited about as a child, it's time to bring yourself to the present day. To do this, my favorite exercise is to wander a bookstore when you have an hour or so to see what genres you are drawn to. What topics? What books?

When you get to the bookstore (or the bookstore's website), pay attention to where you go first. What topics excite you? Write them down! Even small ideas that seem trivial can actually be very telling. Did you love Harry Potter as a child and get excited when you see that book cover? Write it down. Were you obsessed with home makeover shows? Add it to the list! No matter how small, silly, or insignificant it is, be sure to add this topic to your list. When you look at the list at the very end, you may be amazed at the dots you are able to connect—both backward and forward.

Challenge yourself to find books that you would purchase (don't worry, you don't actually have to purchase them). Dig deep beyond just the genres, though. What specific titles catch your eye? Is there something that you've always wanted to learn how to do? Or did you come across a topic that just gives you that glow in your stomach, and you know that book was meant for you? Lean into your emotions here. They will tell you so much.

It will surprise no one that the first place that I go when I get into a bookstore is the self-help section. I used to be self-conscious about going over there, but now that my confidence has grown, I will spend hours flipping through those books. I am so inspired by other women's journeys, and I will take any advice that they can give me to enhance my own experience.

Explore College Course Catalogs

Just like with visiting a bookstore, the next step for helping you to discover some of your passion as an adult can be uncovered by taking a few minutes to flip through a college catalog. Now hear me out: just like you aren't buying books at the bookstore, you're not planning to register for classes (at least not yet!). You are still exploring topics, trying to focus on what areas truly get you excited and eager to learn more.

If you could go back to school right now, what would you go for? What would you tell the eighteen-year-old version of yourself to explore more? In my photography life, I was doing a high school senior session with a teen girl a few weeks ago. She told me she was going to North Carolina to study business, and I fangirled over her. Yes, that is exactly what I would do if I were eighteen again! Business lights me up, and I wish I had realized that earlier. Again, I have no regrets about the way things worked out, but knowing that I had a passion for business would have helped me make some different decisions in my life.

I don't know about you, but every quarter, I receive a course catalog in the mail for local continuing education in neighboring towns. The courses being offered aren't college courses but more hobby-level introductory classes for beginners. This is a great place to start! Flip through a catalog if you get a similar one, and circle anything that makes you go, "Huh, that would be cool." This was the exact process I used to realize that photography was still something that I wanted to learn more about but hadn't made the time to while my family was growing. I actually signed up for the introductory photography class through continuing education, and a few years later, that class was one of my inspirations to turn my passion into a business!

By hopping on to a local college website, you can also look at their course catalogs for undergraduates, which usually provide you with a ton of introductory courses. Challenge yourself to "decide" which course you would invest in if you had to choose one. What topic excites you the most? Which focus area are you drawn to? What specific class piques your interest?

Examine Job Listings

Finally, take some time to look at job listings. Again, you're not necessarily shopping for a new job, just like you weren't actually enrolling in a class. But what job would you be interested in applying for? What catches your eye? If you find a job that you would be interested in applying for, what skills are you missing that would make you a highly qualified candidate?

When I was first considering leaving my full-time teaching job, I went through the exercise of looking at jobs that I could potentially apply for. I found one that I was excited about: being a curriculum coordinator at a local college. I read the job description and realized that it required a background in professional development delivery. I had never run any professional development as a classroom teacher, so I added that to my MAP Book as something I may want to seek out to make myself a more qualified candidate for the future.

As I thought more deeply about applying for that specific job, I had a few realizations while I sat on it for a few days. The first was that I was really hesitant to have to work twelve months a year for the same pay that I made as a teacher. I could work ten months, have summers off with my kids, and make the same money. I also began to think about my time freedom and realized that working this job would mean before and after-school care for my kids would be mandatory, and I'd be commuting an additional thirty minutes each way per day into a big city. These were all major turn-offs for me that I don't think I would have discovered if I hadn't done this exercise. This exercise helped me to clarify what I was looking for in a job and realize that I wanted something that gave me more flexibility with my time, not less.

Take some time in the next week to try one of these exercises. I actually recommend not doing them all at once; give your ideas time to settle and marinate a little bit. You'd be surprised at how much clarity these insights might shed on potential passion pursuits!

Create a Life Experiences List

Most of my clients over the years have had a bucket list or a life experiences list in one form or another. I first created a life experience list before I had kids, when I was wanting to collect all of the dreams that I had in one place.

If you've never created a life experiences list, I strongly recommend it. It may help draw out some passion areas that you hadn't expected and, like the last exercise, clarify for you how you want to invest your time and energy. Whenever I work with a client to create a life experiences list, we often find that the first thirty or so items are the easiest to come up with. After that, things get trickier! The first thirty really are those big life experiences: get married, graduate from college, have kids, pay off my mortgage, go on vacation in Hawaii. But when you get past those big ones, ideas tend to slow down.

Here are some booster ideas to think about:
- Places you want to travel to
- Skills you want to have
- Processes that you want to witness or participate in (jury duty)
- Challenges that you want to complete (thirty days without sugar, run a 5K in a month, whole thirty challenge, write for thirty days)
- Classes you want to take
- People you want to meet
- Financial goals

Remember, everyone's life experiences list looks different. Imagine your-self in your later years, reflecting on a life well-lived. What are you glad that you accomplished or experienced? What regrets do you have? Use these ideas as inspiration for your life experience list. All of the ideas, passions, and goals that you are uncovering during this process will help you to create your action plan for living your dream life.

Some Common Mom Struggles

Before you start exploring some of your passions, it is important to pause to talk through a few struggles that busy moms face when they think about investing time and energy into their own passions. If any of these resonate with you, you are not alone, and these obstacles are not insur-mountable. You just need to take the time to think through them, get creative, and be open-minded to the journey.

Struggle #1: I don't have time.
The struggle that I hear most from busy moms is that they don't have time to invest in their own passion areas. Mama, I get it. Time is critical when you are juggling work, partnerships, finances, kids' soccer sched-ules, and flu shot appointments. But I challenge you with this: what time could you give this passion area?

Let's say that you discover you are very interested in the idea of real estate. You have a stable income and aren't looking to become a real estate agent tomorrow, but you're just curious about the process. Maybe you think it could be a neat thing to get into when your kids are a little older and college costs are on the horizon. Where could that fit into your life? Do you need to take the real estate exam right now? Heck no. Could you make a Pinterest board at your son's soccer practice? Heck yes. Could you take some books out of the library to flip through at night be-fore going to bed? Definitely. Would it be possible to have coffee with a friend who is a real estate agent one morning after drop off? You betcha!

You only need to have the time that you want to have for this passion area. When I took my first photography class, my daughter was six weeks old. Six weeks old! My busy days consisted of nursing schedules, sleep deprivation, and trying to remember to feed myself. But when I saw that class, I asked my husband to prioritize being home on Wednesday nights so I could drag myself to the local high school and learn the basics of how a DSLR camera works. Was I rolling in free time? Nope! But it was an hour and a half a week that turned into a lucrative career five years later.

Look at this book. When clients and friends asked me how I had time to write it during my photography busy season, nonetheless, I admitted that I just made the time for it. I committed to writing thirty minutes a day and stuck to it. There were definitely days that I did not want to do it, and I skipped a few days here and there throughout the process. But at the end of the day, I have a draft of a book that will change moms' lives with the same investment I could have given watching a reality TV show.

Time will forever be a struggle, Mama. I hate to be the one to tell you that. It's up to you to decide how you want to invest your time and get creative if you truly want to be, to invest some of that time back into yourself and into your future.

Struggle #2: I've already pursued everything that I am passionate about.
If you find yourself resonating with this sentiment, my biggest advice for you is to pause and go back to the exercises in this chapter. Everyone is passionate about something, and I have never met anyone who has done all of the things on their bucket list and is just sitting around now.

Go back through some of these exercises if you are in the right frame of mind for it. I would also recommend walking away from this chapter and coming back to it. If you are having an off day and not feeling in a high vibe state, today may not be the day to tackle this.

Do you remember my "weird" passions as a kid—organizing, planning, writing and reading? Those still count! Maybe you love the idea of learning how to cook or planning trips or budgeting. Do not discount any ideas because you think they are lame. They only have to excite you, no one else.

Take some time to notice how you feel when other people share their experiences. When you are scrolling on social media, do you ever get that twinge of "That's so cool, I wish I could have her life?" Pay attention to those feelings! I noticed that I was having a lot of those feelings when I looked at local photographers. I would hire them to do my family portraits and then think about how cool their job was. I did that for actual years before I realized that I could do that too. Those feelings definitely are not fun, but they can be informative!

Finally, be sure to use your resources. On my website, you will find a list of passions that moms can explore to jumpstart your own thinking. You may just need someone to jog your memory. Pinterest can also be a great place to explore hobby and passion ideas that you may be interested in pursuing.

Struggle #3: My kids are involved in so many activities that there isn't room for me to have activities of my own.

Honestly, I totally can relate to this sentiment, and I believe moms should always give themselves grace if they are in a season of "busy." But if you are always in this season, I would strongly suggest that you take a moment to reflect on that. Do you want your children's passions to forever prevent you from having your own? Would they want that for you?

I can not tell you how many clients I have worked with whose children are now teenagers and are shedding some of their childhood passions. All of a sudden, these moms are finding themselves with time on their hands, and they panic. To them, it felt like a day just came when, all of a sudden, they were not incredibly busy, and they had nothing to fill the void.

Now, I hate to be dramatic, but take a moment to ask yourself, what are you going to do when your youngest child moves out? Who are you going to be when you are an empty nester? I really encourage you to think about your dream life vision. What is the version of you that your grown children are really going to be excited to come visit?

Your children are always watching. I want to model that I have my own passions outside of them. Of course, my children are my priority, but I want them to see me making myself my priority, too. It is the whole airplane analogy of putting your oxygen mask on first before you help others. I need to show them it is possible to be a mom, have passions, and live a life that I love every single day.

Remember that this exploration of passions is really just a scavenger hunt at this point. You want to be open to any and all things, and you may start to notice as you are creating your list that you notice passion areas more. For example, a mom in our group coaching session shared that she always wanted to learn how to do her hair really well. Then another mom chimed in that she actually wanted to learn how to do her own make-up really well. The energy on the call lit up, and everyone was furiously writing in their notebooks as we went down that rabbit hole together. Don't be afraid of rabbit holes. That's sometimes where our best ideas live!

> **You can download a free template to create your own three-year action plan by checking out the book resources on my website: www.sharonlegercoaching.com**

LET'S MAKE A PLAN!

Write the following lists in your MAP Book:
- "Things That I Am Interested In"
- "Things I Was Passionate About As A Child/Teenager"
- "Life Experiences List"
- Take the time to go through each passion area exercise and add to your list.

Up Next

In Chapter Ten, you will:
- Brainstorm what you want your life to look like in three years.
- Plan backward to imagine what it could look like in two years, one year, six months.
- Create distinct action steps to help you bring that vision to life.
- Learn ways to upgrade your life today so you can start living a life you love right now!

CHAPTER TEN

Creating Your Dream Life Action Plan

Becky was so excited for our second-to-last meeting. After months of working together, it was finally time to start creating the action plan that was going to fast-track her to her dream life. We had spent countless hours together, getting organized, crafting her dream life vision, implementing time maximization strategies, and identifying her core values. All of this hard work was about to culminate into one tangible plan, and I don't know who was more excited—me or Becky!

As a Type A planner, I had gone through versions of creating a life plan for years. When I fully committed to the idea that I was going to change my life in the next three years, this exercise took on a whole new meaning. Instead of being able to sit down in a coffee shop for an hour and crank this out, this took several sessions of taking breaks, walking away from it, reflecting, and coming back to the process.

I don't tell you these things to intimidate you but rather to normalize the process and the feelings that you may encounter. Creating a three-year action plan truly changed my life and helped me grow from a stressed-out, overwhelmed teacher to a thriving, small-business mama. There was a time in my life when I honestly believed that I would never have time or financial freedom. Now, I have both. I would highly recommend diving into this chapter with an open heart and an open mind and see where it leads you!

Before we get too far down the road, let's take a moment to pause, reflect, and see how far we've come. Up until this point, you have:

- Defined personal growth and correlated it to making your dream life a reality
- Created a system to keep you organized
- Assessed your current context and identified areas of strength and challenge
- Maximized the time that you have on the things that matter most
- Identified your core values
- Set goals and measured your progress
- Found your passions
- Established positive habits and systems to help you achieve your goals

Now, it's time to put all of these things into action and create your three-year, dream life action plan. To me, this is the most exciting part of your journey. Mama, it's been work to get to this point. But this is where all of the things start to come together, and you'll begin to see the magic in the process. I strongly suggest reading through this entire chapter, then coming back to revisit it in smaller chunks to put this process into action. And as always, finding a friend or a supportive coach can be the difference between success and overwhelm during this part of your journey.

Why Three Years?

One question that I am often asked is: why is your action plan for three years, not one, five, or ten? Believe it or not, there actually is some solid reasoning behind this. In my opinion, one year is too soon to really make a huge life change—like a career shift, a family change, or anything else life-altering. If you're serious about making progress toward your dream life in a big way, a year is simply not enough time. To set yourself up with that expectation at the very beginning seems unhelpful.

On the flip side, five or ten years is just too dang far away. You're a tired mom who is often overwhelmed by the pure magnitude of the day-to-day. Can you seriously picture what your life is going to be like in five years? Personally, I struggle with this. When my oldest was five, I could reasonably picture where life would be when she was eight. But to imagine her at ten or fifteen years old? That was further than my imagination could realistically bring me.

So, three years it is! Before I even begin this process, I like to do quick math to write down how old I will be, how old my husband will be, and how old my kids will be three years from now.

Designing Your Roadmap to Your Dream Life

Step 1: Brainstorm What You Want Your Life To Look Like In Three Years

In Chapter Four, we spent a lot of time dissecting and creating our dream life vision. That is going to come back in full force right now. Without looking back at it, challenge yourself to set aside an hour to just re-brainstorm that dream life and where you would be exactly three years from today.

For me, that initially looked like a list in my MAP Book. I was sitting on a dock overlooking Highland Lake in New Hampshire as the sun came up. My husband was making breakfast happen with the kiddos, and I always prefer a change from my daily scenery to dream big. In my MAP Book, I wrote at the top, "What I Want My Life To Look Like Three Years From Now." Then, I set a timer for ten minutes and just brainstormed a list of everything I could think of.

In some areas, I was able to be super specific. I wanted to go on vacation for a month every year, I wanted our student loans paid off, and I wanted my business to bring in six figures. Those things felt tangible to me. But there were other concepts that felt less tangible. For example, I wanted to have time freedom and financial freedom. Honestly, I couldn't get more specific than that at the time because I didn't know exactly what would lead me to that result. But I knew that was the desired outcome, so I added it to the dang list, even though I wasn't sure how I would make it happen.

Step 2: Refine
After taking a week or two away from this list in my MAP Book, I came back to it with fresh eyes. Sitting in my basement with a piece of chart paper and a pile of markers (former teacher perks), I grouped all of the ideas that I had out on the dock into categories. The categories that I came up with were financial, physical, mental, family/marriage, and work-related. From there, I took each of my top five categories and boiled them down into a phrase or affirmation that I would always be working toward.

Here's what I came up with::
- Healthy Mindset
- Thriving Business
- Work/Life Balance
- Financial Freedom
- Empowering Moms

While there are definitely more categories in my life that I want to consciously grow in, these five were the ones that really came to the top. These were the five areas that I wanted to focus my three-year action plan around most. From there, I create a mind map on a large sheet of paper. On my mind map, I used the above categories to continue to brainstorm what would be my rough goals in that area.

For example, work/life balance. What was important to me? I brainstormed the idea of rest, routines, schedules, and how I show up as a mom and as a wife. Does that mean that I don't want to be a great aunt, daughter, sister? Nope. It just isn't going to be my main focus right now since my kiddos are still fairly early in their childhood, and this is where I want to spend most of my conscious efforts.

Let's break down another category together: a healthy mindset. For me, the important things in regard to a healthy mindset are gratitude, using my joy list, eating right, doing daily affirmations, and meditation.

Someone else may choose to focus on a healthy, strong body. What may be important to them could be nutrition, consistent workouts, energy levels, and confidence. What the category is, or the aspects that are important to you are deeply personal, and there is definitely not a one-size-fits-all here.

Right now, take the time to do your very first brainstorm. Maybe you have to break it up into a few different sessions because you don't have an hour to spare. That is more than okay. The reason not everyone does this is because it is WORK, and it is HARD. But if you want to live a life that you want your children to emulate one day, you need to do something different than you're currently doing, Mama. You need to do the dang work. So don't make an excuse that you don't have an hour and then go scroll Instagram for twenty minutes. Make it happen!

Step 3: Create Distinct Action Steps

Alright, Mama, here it is: the crucial step. Other than actually implementing the work, this is the key. I knew after I created the categories that I wanted to focus on I needed concrete steps that would be accomplished at various points to get me to my end destination. To do that, I created the chart on the next page:

On the left-hand side, you see the five different categories that I chose to focus my efforts on. Underneath each, I wrote the three to five things that were most important to me in that category for the next three years. After that, each column represents a different milestone: what I can start doing today, where I will be two months from today, where I will be in one year, two years, and three years.

What is important?	What can I start doing TODAY?	60 Days	1 Year	2 Years	3 Years
Work/Life balance · Routines · Schedule · Rest · Wife · Mom	✓ Early wake-ups ✓ Start weekly family routines ✓ Theme days for work	✓ Decide on weekday sheeting & eating days (short every other weekend · Tu & W)	· Family-first schedule set weekends/month · Vacations planned & out · Maine vacation in July · Excited to go to work every day	· Family-first schedule, 2 weekends/month · Overnight trip with each girl · Work 5 days/week · Excited to go to work every day	· Family-first schedule · Work no weekends · Overnight trip with each girl once a year/Maine vac. · Work 4 days/week · Excited to go to work every day
Healthy Mindset · Gratitude · Joy List · Eating Right · Affirmations · Guided Meditations	✓ Write out high vibe routine ✓ Plan 21 day fix	✓ Plan meals & snacks ✓ Make guided meditation playlist - get account	· Workout daily · Daily gratitude · Planned rest · Mindful eating · Daily meditation & affirmations · High vibe routine	· Workout daily · Daily gratitude · Planned rest · Mindful eating · Daily meditation & affirmations · High vibe routine	· Feel in control of my mindset · Feel confident in my body · Positive outlook · No more SADD · Grateful for all that I have
Thriving Business · Less Sessions · Marketing · Increased income · Client Experience · Outsource editing	✓ Work to minimize photography tasks to maximize coaching ✓ Map out content through March	· High value tasks to bring in the right clients · Find an editor	· Price increase · 2 minis/year · 12 sessions/month · Bring home $80k · Add to client experience · Commit to editing outsource	· Price increase · 12 sessions booked each month · Bring home $100k	
Empowering Moms · Services · Community · Lead magnets · Passive income · Marketing · Education	✓ Create content calendar	· Plan future projects · First passive income product is prepared · Have PD website	· Ready to launch first round of group coaching · Planning 1st PD retreat · 3 1:1 clients · Passive income streams established (course) · Book outline complete	· Launch 2nd round of group coaching · Have 12 1:1 clients · Exceed photography income · Continuing with passive income streams	· Spend 1/3 of my time working on my book · Coaching more than shooting · Multiple income streams · Passive income · Hit 6 figures with coaching
Financial Freedom · Student loan · Retirement · College · Mortgage		· Budget	· Meet with Scott to decide on our next steps · Replan future financial projection based on Scott recommendations · College is being 50% funded	· Student loan paid off · Retirement maxed out · 5 years away from vaca. house · College is being 50% funded	· 3 years away from vaca. house · Rsch. 2nd properties · Retirement maxed out · College is being 50% funded

When you're looking at your blank chart (which you can find on the resources page of my website), I promise you, you will probably initially have feelings of overwhelm. Know that is completely normal, and we'll chat more in the next section about how to overcome that. But your first step really is to skip over all of the columns and go straight to the three years from now, at the far right.

Why? Because you've already done this work! On your list, you have already visualized where you and your family will be in three years. Let's look at the first row as an example. For work/life balance, I know that three years from now, I want:
- Family-first schedule (working when my kids are at school and my husband is at work, prioritizing their activities over my work)
- Do not work on weekends
- Overnight trip with each girl, once a year
- Maine vacation for at least three weeks a year, if not four
- Work four days a week
- Excited to go to work every day

Some of these are general, some of them are specific. But that is where I want to be in three years. Now, it's time to do some backward planning and design. If, in three years, I want to be there, where do I need to be in two years? It would probably need to look something like this:
- Family-first schedule, two weekends a month
- Overnight trip with each girl
- Maine vacation
- Work five days a week
- Excited to go to work every day

As you can see, I'm making progress toward those goals, but I'm not 100% of the way there—maybe 75% of the way there.

You know what's coming next. What would one year from now have to look like—50% of the way there?

- Have set shooting and editing days, certain days blocked off for my family
- Vacations planned out in advance
- Day trip with each girl
- Maine vacation for at least two weeks
- Work five days a week
- Excited to go to work every day

Again, you're really just reverse engineering here to figure out what you need to do in the near future to set yourself up to achieve your dream life in the next three years. The second to last step is to think about what you need to start doing in the next sixty days to make the one-year milestone happen. For me, that looked like just deciding which days would be work days and which days would be family days. That's it. Easy peasy. Probably took one conversation with my husband and fifteen minutes, max. Done.

From there, the very last step is to think about what you could do right now to take a step toward your first milestone. These are usually the prerequisite steps that need to happen, more the administrative tasks if you will. For me, that looked like getting back to early wake-ups so that I could get ahead on my work days, start weekly family routines that we could get consistent with, and then theme my days for work so that I really started to understand how my time was spent. Again, I was able to do those steps fairly quickly and already felt like I was making big progress toward that first milestone.

After completing the first category, it was time to move on to the second and think through this same process in the context of a healthy mindset. I would say, if you wanted to sit down and do this whole process, maybe on a personal growth weekend retreat or something similar, it would probably take you a solid three hours to map it all out.

But then step back and look at it. This is your guide, your cheat sheet, your map to your dream life. You have invested so much time in yourself to get to this place, and the finish line is right there. You got this, Mama!

Common Struggles

I was so pumped up the first time I did this process. Seeing everything laid out in such a tangible way was so motivating and inspiring. That's why I was surprised when I began to use it with clients that I began to see some struggles that popped up. Let's take the time to address those here in case you find yourself in a similar headspace as you're going through this work.

Struggle #1: This feels overwhelming.
You bet it does! Especially at the beginning, this can be a super over-whelming task. But remember, that's why it is structured the way that it is. If you take the time to really brainstorm your dream life vision and what you want things to look like in three years, things will flow after that, I promise!

One strategy you can use to counter the feeling of overwhelm is to not sit down to do this task all at once, especially not with a strict deadline. Commit to one step of the process, and that's it. For example, maybe the first time, you'll plan to just write down the list for your dream life and save the mind map for another day. That will make the whole process feel less daunting. And as an added bonus, you'll have time to reflect on the work you've done and come back to it with fresh eyes. You may be surprised about the ideas you want to add or subtract once you have given your ideas a chance to breathe.

Finally, just because you're feeling overwhelmed doesn't mean you should stop. This is probably the biggest reason clients have for giving up on their three-year action plan. I promise this is where the magic lies, though. Do you want your kids to give up when they get overwhelmed? Definitely not. Set an example for them, create small goals, and get support when you need it.

Struggle #2: I don't have time.

If I had a dollar every time a client told me that they didn't have the time to do this work, I wouldn't have to worry about financial freedom any-more! Next to overwhelm, this is probably the second most popular thing that clients struggle with when creating their three-year action plan.

As we discussed in Chapter Five, we all have the same amount of time, it's just how we choose to prioritize it and utilize it that makes the difference. If you truly don't believe you have the time to make this happen, you may want to ask yourself a hard question: do you really want to do this work? That's a gut punch. If you truly do want to create your dream life vision in the next three years, you are going to have to work for it. There is no magic secret or pill you can take. It's hard work, sweat equity, and sacrifice.

My recommendation would be to set aside sacred time for this exercise. If you want to make one big work session happen, take the afternoon off from work. Yup, I said it. I left teaching with fifty-six sick days in the bank. Why? Because I wasn't prioritizing myself. Each of those fifty-six sick days represents to me a day that I didn't put myself or my family first. You can bet that I regret that. So do it, take the day off, go to your favorite coffee shop, and work through this exercise. Consider it your first bold move toward the future you that is confident, fearless, and doesn't hide behind excuses of "there is no time."

What if taking an afternoon off from work is not an option? See if you can swap an afternoon of childcare with another mom or ask your support system for help. Mama, I promise you, you do need this. You just won't realize it until you've taken the time. Just like we want our kids to ask for help when they need it, you need to ask for help when you need it, too.

No afternoons off and no support system? No worries! Set a date with yourself. Think about when your kids are in bed, either early or late, and make this work happen then. Again, if you truly want to prioritize yourself, you need to remove other things, such as passively scrolling on your phone or watching TV. Personal growth requires a time investment, so if you can't find bonus time, use the time you already have more strategically.

Finally, one more hard truth, Mama. If you find yourself in a season where you truly don't have a moment to yourself, this might not be the right time to start your personal growth journey. If every minute and every second of every day is already accounted for, you may need to work on creating space before you can truly start strategically taking action toward your dream life.

That can be a frustrating reality for moms because once you have a taste of your dream life, you're ready to start chasing it. But if you are caring for a sick loved one or have just brought home a new baby, you may want to set a reminder in your MAP Book or on your calendar to come back to this in six months to reassess if you're ready to start doing some of this heavy lifting.

There is no shame in this. I know it's frustrating, but as moms, we also know that we aren't always the ones who are in charge of our schedules. So be honest, patient, and gracious with yourself. You'll get there, I promise!

Struggle #3: I don't even know what I want my dream life to look like.
This was me six years ago. I have had a dream life vision since I was a teenager. I wanted to graduate from college, get a great job, meet the perfect guy, get married, buy a house, and have babies. All those things happened, and in 2016, after my second (and last) baby was born, my list ran out. There was no vision past this point, and it was overwhelming.

I knew that I wanted something different, but I didn't know what that looked like. If you feel this in your soul, Mama, you are not alone! My suggestion to you is to not get too caught up in the specifics of your dream life but ask yourself broader questions. What do you want your job to do for you? What kind of mom do you want to be? When you start asking these broader questions, you can worry about just the what, not the how.

When I was in this place, I was able to identify that I wanted time freedom. As an extremely organized, efficient person, it bothered me that no matter how much work I got done during the school day as a teacher, I still had to be there until 3:55 PM each day, no matter what. My time was not my own, and I resented that. So, in 2016, I was able to identify that I wanted to create my own schedule, be able to put my kids on the bus every day and see the sunshine in the winter. Of course, I had no idea HOW I was going to do any of those things. I just knew that I wanted them. And for right now, that's enough.

Once you have asked those more general questions and brainstormed some responses, I would suggest walking away from the list for at least a few days, if not a week (make a note in your MAP Book to come back to it!). Start to notice when you see someone else doing something with their life that you are envious of. I had friends who would meet up for lunch on a random Tuesday. I was jealous. I saw family members getting out of debt...I wanted that! Force yourself to look beyond that initial jealousy reaction and dig deeper into why you had a reaction. What you want for your life might be lying there, right underneath the surface.

Still feeling stuck? Revisit Chapter Four and go through some of the exercises again to help you work through and elaborate on your dream life vision until it makes you feel genuinely excited.

Struggle #4: I don't have enough ideas.
A lot of moms in my first coaching group wanted to make a career shift,

so we spent a lot of time discussing that. In a 1:1 session with one of those moms, Shannon, she admitted, almost guiltily, that she didn't want to make a career change. She was happy with her work, felt fulfilled, and didn't feel the need to make any changes.

And you know what? That is great! There is no one-size-fits-all, and living your dream life doesn't mean a job switch, a partner switch, a new baby, or a lifestyle shake-up. You can be quite happy with the life you're living and make smaller changes to get it closer to your ideal life.

Shannon knew a job change wasn't for her. But she did notice, since having kids, that she really has no hobbies of her own. She wanted her sons to see her engaged with things that she is passionate about that have nothing to do with work or parenting. So we worked together to think about what those hobbies might be and how that would look in her dream life vision.

When clients come to me without "enough" ideas for their action plan, I encourage them to walk away from it for a bit. Again, you want to spend time noticing what you think about, what you're envious of, and what piques your interest on Pinterest. In conversations with other people, notice if your inner voice goes, "That's so cool. I wish I knew how to rock climb." That is your inner mentor nudging you toward a new passion area. Listen to it, write it down, and see how it feels in a few weeks!

Struggle #5: I have too many ideas!

If you're anything like me, you can often find yourself in a situation where you want to do all the things and do them right now! Just like the mom who struggles with not enough ideas, I encourage you to follow a similar process. Write all of your ideas down and then walk away. What are the ideas that keep coming back to you? What do you think about at night before you fall asleep? Which idea lights that fire in your belly and gets you pumped up so much that you can physically feel it? Those are the ideas you want to focus on.

Just because you have a lot of ideas doesn't mean that you have to act on them all. For example, I am super interested in real estate. I follow a few real estate gurus on Instagram and can often get lost in a Zillow rabbit hole on a rainy Friday afternoon. The idea of getting my real estate license excites me. That being said, I also know in my gut that it's not the right time. Why? One reason, I don't want to spend more time away from home. Two, I don't want to split my attention again while my kids are still young. Maybe this would be a cool thing to pursue later, but right now, it's not the priority. And three, there are things that excite me more, like writing this book. Because of these things, I've left real estate on the list, and maybe someday, I'll come back to it.

If you're finding yourself drowning in ideas, another suggestion would be to put them in a prioritized list. If you could wave a magic wand and only make three of these wishes come true, which three would they be? Those are the ones you want to focus your energy on.

If you find that making that list is challenging, try talking to your support person or a personal growth coach to just do a brainstorming session. Sometimes, having another person's perspective can help you see the reality of a situation, especially if you're the kind of person who can get over eager and idealistic quickly. By presenting your thought process to a trusted person, they may be able to give you feedback that you hadn't considered.

Finally, remember that you do not need to finalize all of your plans in this exercise in one day. Create a draft, even if it is a long draft, and work over the course of a few weeks to narrow it down and focus in. You will get there, I promise!

Struggle #6: I don't really think anything is going to change or get better.

The final common struggle is the mindset that nothing in your life can change. You may have a little devil on your shoulder, reminding you that you carry the health insurance for your family, so you can never leave your job. Or that if you don't make X amount of money, your family won't survive.

Been there, done that! Once my husband and I were finally past the early teacher paychecks, we got used to a certain lifestyle level. When an opportunity popped up for me to work part-time, a mentor teacher encouraged me to pursue it. I balked at the idea, thinking there was no way I would be able to pull that off. That weekend, when I hesitantly presented it to my husband, he shot it down. Why? Not because he didn't believe in me. But because we truly believed that we could not figure the financial part out.

The next day, my mentor teacher asked what I had decided. I told her there was no way we could make it happen financially, even though I desperately wanted the time with my kids. She challenged me to sit down and actually crunch the numbers to see where we landed. It was a Friday, so I spent Saturday afternoon creating a spreadsheet and really running through all of our options. By doing that, I was able to see gaps that would happen if we no longer needed full-time daycare and lifestyle adjustments that we could make that would make this transition possible. On Monday morning, I applied for the job. Just like that, the first leap toward my dream life vision had been accomplished.

All that being said, I realize that I had a lot of privilege in being able to make the decisions that I have made over the past few years. I have a partner who is happy with his work, brings home a consistent paycheck, and carries our health insurance. If any of those circumstances were different, I realize there is a chance that my dream life would need to look a little different. But if I had let the fear of financial instability paralyze me, I never would have gotten to where I am today.

So, how do you overcome this mindset? First, figure out what is holding you back. Is it financial fear? Is it fear of failure? Does the change of status terrify you? Are you worried about what your loved ones might think? All of these are valid fears, and the first step to overcoming them is to acknowledge what they are. Remember when I first talked to my husband about making a career change, and he immediately shut it down? If I hadn't been prodded by my colleague to really examine the scenario, that would have been that.

Once you have identified your fears, it's time to take it one step further and really examine them. Play out the scenario. What would it mean to take a pay cut? What would that actually mean to your budget? Talk to your loved ones. Maybe you wouldn't be able to afford daycare, but do they have any ideas? You would be surprised how much others want to help. You just have to speak up.

Embarking On Your Dream Life

If you are still with me, you just created your three-year dream life action plan–CONGRATULATIONS! This is a huge deal, Mama. Just by looking at the previous section, you can see how many obstacles you have overcome and the huge amount of work, dedication, and passion that went into this process.

But now what? Your next step is to set a reminder on your calendar and walk away from your three-year action plan for a day or two. Let it simmer, let it settle. If you have someone in your life like a partner, close friend, or coach/mentor, share it with them in a few days.

Ask questions like:

- Am I missing any steps to get me from point A to point B?
- Am I pushing myself enough?
- Am I pushing myself too far?

This last question is especially challenging. When I look at the column for three years from now, I always get butterflies. Why? Because that column scares the crap out of me, and it feels overwhelming right in this moment. If you feel similarly, you're on the right path. Remember, it's three full years from now—1,095 days from today. That is so much time. Even looking at your kiddos, three years ago probably feels like a lifetime ago. Keep that in mind. Don't limit yourself by setting safe goals. This is not the time or the place for it.

> "Remember, this three-year action plan is a roadmap, not a rule book. Give yourself permission to tweak it and make adjustments as needed."

After you have done some reflecting on your action plan, it's time to really zero in on that first column. After all, a marathon starts at the starting line, and that is where you are right now. What do you need to start doing today?

When I look at my action plan, I can quickly see the first few steps that need to happen in each priority area. For example, for financial freedom, I need to set an appointment with our financial advisor, then make changes to our budget based on his recommendations. That's not a huge action item, but it has to be done in order to begin to make progress.

For a thriving business, I need to begin to think about the next calendar year so that I can start to strategize and reflect on how I want to spend my time. While this seems super proactive, it is honestly better to do it now while next year still feels abstract. I can look at a somewhat blank calendar and have the white space to dream up the ideal balance. That being said, there are some other smaller actions that come along with it. I need to discuss vacation plans with my husband and my family to make sure that those important things are on the calendar. I also need to do some research on my children's school district website to find out important dates, school vacations, and when different events are so that I can be as present as possible.

Those are the action items that you want to start tackling today. You will notice, as you begin to make progress, that your action steps and milestones may change. For example, I booked our family vacation while thinking through my work/life balance because I could not map out my work calendar until I knew exactly when we would be away as a family. So I went ahead and did it. Just like that, I had already accomplished one of the action items on my list for the first year.

Be careful not to get too ahead of yourself, though. The best thing to do would be to set a reminder on your calendar to revisit your three-year action plan once a month to reflect on your progress and figure out what you should be taking action on. Each priority area doesn't need to be acted on each month. During my photography busy season, I am mostly focused on my photography business and work/life balance. But as soon as December hits and photography gets quiet, I shift my focus more to my coaching business for busy moms, my healthy mindset, and financial freedom.

Remember, this three-year action plan is a roadmap, not a rule book. Give yourself permission to tweak it and make adjustments as needed. I purposefully create this document as a Google Doc, and whenever I update it, I just copy and paste the old one onto the first page and add a new date to it. That way, I have a progression, in one document, of the different versions of my action plan. Change is good. That means you are growing and that you are taking action!

Upgrade Your Life Today

Once you have created your three-year action plan and have started to take action steps toward it consistently, you will probably begin to notice a plateau. It does not usually happen until three to six months in when you are slowly taking action but not yet seeing progress. Be wary of this. You do not want to lose momentum, get frustrated, or quit. Remember, if it was easy, everyone would be doing it.

My trick to keeping the momentum alive is to keep going back to that third-year column. That is the vision you want to keep burning in the forefront of your mind. To help you do that, I suggest implementing something that I call "life upgrades." When you look at that column for three years from now, what is something that will be included in that that you could start right now?

For me, when I think of financial freedom, I think of fresh-cut flowers. Haha, what? Yup, whenever I think of being financially free, I think of having fresh-cut flowers in my house because all of my necessities are taken care of. I can spoil myself with something "unnecessary" that makes me happy every time that I look at it. This is an example of a life upgrade in my world. However, instead of waiting for that day to come, I figured out a way to make it happen now. I wanted a small representation of my dream life vision to happen now, and the fact that it smells lovely doesn't hurt anything, either!

So that is what I did. I actually found a local woman who was just starting her own flower business. She cuts fresh flowers from her garden and sells them at the end of her driveway every Sunday morning for $10. Each Sunday, I get in my car, drive up to her house, support a local business, and bring home a visual reminder of what I am working toward. Your action steps don't all have to be sacrifice and hard work. You can indulge yourself in the perks to remind you of what is coming.

There is another benefit to implementing life upgrades right off the bat. Stay with me now: I truly believe that by leaning into what you consider a life upgrade, you are telling the universe that you are serious. That little voice that says, "You shouldn't spend $10 on fresh cut flowers until you have made six figures," is back-handed when you set that mason jar on the table. That is your way of announcing, "Psh, I am so confident that I'll be making six figures that I'm getting ready for that lifestyle now!" In my imagination, that causes the universe to go, "Oh, shoot, she's for real!" and get to work on helping you manifest your dream life vision.

Don't get carried away with this, though. You don't want to blow your life savings or your emergency fund by upgrading your life too quickly. But make a list right now in your notebook of "life upgrades" that you would envision having when you're living your dream life vision. Then, go back through that list and ask yourself: "What is realistic for me now?"

My life upgrade list includes an Audible subscription, fresh cut flowers, a Spotify subscription, buying books whenever I want to, and monthly massages. Obviously, if I did all of those things, it would require at least $150 a month, and that would throw off my financial freedom goals. So I looked at what I could do and settled on $10 flowers weekly and buying one book a month. Those feel like luxuries to me. I appreciate them, and they remind me of all of the abundance coming my way once I put that hard work in. So go ahead, get your list started, and start living aspects of your dream life today.

LET'S MAKE A PLAN!

- Brainstorm what you want your life to look like in three years.
- Download the blank template from the website to plan backward to imagine what it could look like in two years, one year, six months–use the three-year action plan models on my website for inspiration!
- Create distinct action steps to help you bring that vision to life.
- Make a list of three ways you are going to start upgrading your life today.
- Print your action steps chart and post it somewhere you can review it regularly.

Up Next

In the conclusion of this book, you will:

- Discover a summary of each chapter to remind you of the highlights.
- Be prompted to complete an action step based on the content of the chapter to accelerate your growth, even if there are gaps in your journey.

CONCLUSION

Your Dream Life Awaits!

I love to write lists. There is something so therapeutic about being able to check things off, knowing that they have been accomplished and no longer need to take up space in your life. I literally have lists for everything: life goals, groceries, things I need at Target, traditions I want to start with my family.

So, it was a startling reality when I realized that my personal growth was never going to be checked off my list. Don't get me wrong, huge life events get a happy little checkmark of success, but this process is never done. You will never look around and say, "Welp, I did it. I hit my highest potential, I guess I'll go take a nap" (I mean, I sort of did that last Friday, but that is another story). Like exercise, the work will never be done. If you want to maintain your level of success, growth, and positive energy, you need to constantly be evolving, growing, and learning.

This conclusion is not like most book conclusions. To be honest, I usually skip the conclusion because they are typically a watered-down recap of everything you just invested your time in reading—and they are boring, at best. Not this one!

In this final section, we are going to review the biggest ideas of the book and define one concrete action step that you can take in each area to make massive growth toward your dream life. This chapter will be a great way for you to review the content of the book, whether you have just finished it or are coming back to it after some time away.

Let's get into it. In this journey together, we have:

Defined personal growth in relation to your dream life (Chapter One):

In Chapter One, we really dove into the question: what is personal growth? From there, we examined how you can accelerate your progress toward your dream life vision through personal growth activities. Once you have adopted this growth mindset, Mama, there is no stopping you!

Action Step: Take a few moments right now to brainstorm in a notebook what personal growth means to you. Where are you right now on your personal growth journey? Who in your life has leaned into their personal growth and could serve as a mentor to you? There are no right or wrong answers here. Take the time to get all of your thoughts into your MAP Book. This will be interesting to look back on as you progress through your journey.

Created a system to keep you organized and avoid overwhelm (Chapter Two):

Chapter Two was all about creating your MAP Book, a customized notebook system to help you avoid being overwhelmed. One of the main purposes of this system is for you to go from reactive to proactive in motherhood. Have you started this system yet? Do you have a catch-all system that you trust to give you the confidence that nothing is slipping through the cracks?

Action Step: If you brushed over this system and did not take the time to dive deeply into creating your own, take a moment to reconsider. The notebook system is not just a gimmick. I make $0 from you purchasing a 99¢ notebook from Target and setting up your system. I share it with you because it works, and the best part, it can be whatever you need it to be. This system will help you plan your entire quarter—day by day, week by week, and month by month. If you decide that this system is not for you, decide which parts of it resonate with you or what you need in your life. Then, design a way to make sure that those happen—whether it's a Google calendar, a paper planner, a binder system, or a Trello board. If you truly want to make progress on your personal growth journey, you need a way to stay on top of everything else. When you get overwhelmed, your personal growth and your dream life vision will be the first things on the cutting board. We want to avoid that as much as possible.

Assessed where you currently stand (Chapter Three):

If you struggled during this chapter, you are not alone! One of the hardest things to do is to hold up a mirror on your current situation and truly reflect on what is working and what is not working. However, doing this work in a strategic, authentic way is what is going to give you the power to take action. Nothing is going to get better if you don't actively work to make it better. By seeing the gap areas in your life, you are acknowledging that growth is needed, and then you can strategize the type of support that you need to close the gap.

Action Step: If you haven't already, go ahead and print off twelve reflection wheels so that you can quickly and easily tape them into your MAP

Book at the beginning of each month. No matter what day it is today, take the time to tape in a reflection wheel and assess where you stand today in each category. Toss a date on the top and decide on two to three action steps that will help you make progress over the next month. Put a reminder in your monthly page in your MAP Book to come back to this exercise next month to see your growth.

Designed your dream life vision (Chapter Four):

As the author, I am probably not supposed to have a favorite chapter (isn't it kind of like having a favorite child?), but the work that we did in the chapter on dream life vision sets my soul on fire. This is where everything comes together, where you create white space to dream, create, and plan in a way that you may not have done since you were a teenager, dreaming of leaving behind your parents' house.

While this chapter is my favorite, it probably is simultaneously the most challenging chapter. Thus, the list of struggles that clients have encountered in this particular area.

Action Step: If you are reading this book at the same pace as your personal growth journey transpires, this exercise may have been done a long time ago. Look around. Do you see evidence of your life today that encapsulates your dream life vision? Is there a visual representation of your dream life vision in your closet, on your mirror, as the background of your desktop computer at work?

Now here is a hard question. Does your dream life vision fire you up? I mean, does it really get you excited for the version of your life that lies ahead on your personal growth journey? Be honest with yourself here. This is where a lot of clients tend to fall apart. They create a dream life vision that they think they should want or just recreate a journey that someone else has taken. But that vision is not going to fire you up and cause you to jump out of bed every morning. So if your dream life vision causes you to casually shrug your shoulders and think, "Meh, that could be kinda cool," you need a new vision, Mama!

It is hard because you really can not rush this work. Your dream life vision may come easily to you if you're lucky, but if you're in the majority, this is heavy lifting. It is hard to push past the constraints of your current reality to imagine what life could be. But just like a muscle, you need to work your imagination to imagine how good things could be.

When I first started my personal growth journey, I thought that I wanted to open a used book store for kids. While that dream life vision still excites me, I realized it was not the right time in my life to pursue that particular dream. I knew it would mean long hours away from my family, and that was not what I wanted right now or in the next ten years. So I had to do the heartbreaking work of accepting that reality and then being open to other opportunities that could allow me to leave teaching in a way that felt safe and empowering, with more time with my family.

You truly need multiple ways every day to remind you of your dream life vision. There was a point where I had a vision board, daily mantras, and a password at work that reminded me of my resignation date. In order to open your mind up to the possibility of growth, you need to remind your brain multiple times a day of what you are working for.

Maximize the time that you do have on the things that matter most (Chapter Five):

Remember, Mama, you don't need a new planner or to wake up at 3:00 AM or to do anything crazy to manage your time. Actually, you don't need more time at all—what, to do MORE things? No, you need to maximize the time that you already have to make it work for you. How do you do that? First, identify where your time is going. Then, decide what activities are moving you closer to your dream life vision and which activities are moving you away. Slowly, over time, replace activities that are not providing you with any growth with activities that are. Switch your entertainment podcast over to a personal growth audiobook while you are folding laundry. Instead of scrolling Instagram in front of the TV one night a week, use that time to explore your passion areas. Replace a happy hour with co-workers with an accountability partner meetup to discuss your goals and progress. Small changes lead to big results.

Action Step: If you haven't already, start tracking your time today. I literally do not care how you do it. Just make it happen. As busy moms, we really need to question this idea of "busy." When we are in a blind panic about all of the things that need to happen, it is essential for us to pause and question where our time is going. Not all activities are created equal, and a lot of them are actually not worth our time at the end of the day. Do not be afraid to step away from activities that are not truly adding value to your life or the life of your family.

I believe that the COVID pandemic truly helped all of us develop this mindset of time prioritization. COVID cleared all of our calendars for three months. And while that was terrifying at the time, it truly allowed us to look at a sea of empty calendar squares and question what we wanted to put back. Our family left extracurricular activities that we realized we did not actually miss and began to prioritize who got our time and attention. Random kids' birthday parties from the bus? Nope, not today, thanks.

I'm not saying we need a Pandemic 2.0, but the first step to maximizing your time is knowing where it is going. Start there, and the rest will follow.

Living In Alignment with your Core Values (Chapter Six):

While this definitely is not the most challenging exercise on your personal growth journey, you may have been surprised that you struggled with this one a little bit. Look back at Chapter Seven, what are your top five core values? How are you practicing those values each and every day? How are you sharing them with your children in a meaningful way?

Once I identified my top five core values (simplicity, growth, relationships, meaningful work, and alignment), I found that making decisions got a lot easier. If the activity or opportunity that I was considering did not help me in any of these areas, it was not something that I needed to add to my plate (or calendar!). I was able to use this framework to question relationships that had gone stale yet remained ever-present in my life. I used it to think about experiences that I wanted my children to have and how I wanted to show up as a parent.

Action Step: If this exercise occurred a while ago for you, I encourage you to go back to look at the five core values that you identified. Do they still resonate with you? If not, I promise you that this exercise is worth going back to and revisiting. This may even be a good place to bring in your partner if you have not already, to have a conversation about this idea of the core values that you want to communicate in your family.

Challenge yourself to write your five values on a sticky note and stick them to your bathroom mirror. Read them every morning and evening until you have them completely committed to your memory. Explain them to your children when they ask what they are. Use them as a reflection tool to think about how you lived your core values today. Use them as a planning tool to plan how you will honor your core values in the day ahead. Get creative. The sooner you are living in alignment with your core values, the happier you will find yourself being, day to day.

Set goals and measure your progress (Chapter Seven):

Probably the biggest challenge for busy moms is to take all that we have done up until this point, set a tangible goal, and take action from here. Do not fall into this trap! It is not enough to simply imagine what you want your life to look like and hope that the universe sends it your way. In fact, that is my biggest hang-up about the idea of manifestation. Without implementation, it is simply daydreaming.

Action Step: Once you have created your dream life vision, take a step back and ask yourself: What goals do I need to be working toward (on a daily basis) to help me get to this dream life faster?

For example, if you are working toward becoming a certified yoga instructor, your goal might be to confirm your desire to sign up for a year-long training program after you have successfully completed a thirty-day program at your house to be sure that it is right for you. So the goal: complete an at-home thirty-day yoga program. Your action steps might be to register for the program, download the program, put the classes on your calendar, purchase a new mat, and ask a friend if they want to join you for accountability. The goal plus action steps equal big results. Prove to yourself that you can do this!

Established positive habits and systems to help you achieve your goals (Chapter Eight):

Once you have determined what goals will get you from Point A to Point B, it is time to establish those positive habits and systems that will help you to be successful. Unfortunately, it is not enough to set the goals and hope they work out. You can not count on motivation alone. It is the discipline and routine of the habits that is going to move the dial the most for you.

Let's continue to use the yoga instructor example here. If that is the goal, what habits will help you to make sure this happens on autopilot? What would make daily yoga practice so easy that you couldn't say no? Maybe those habits would be an early wake-up, setting your mat up the night before, laying out your yoga clothes, and putting a green X on your calendar every time you successfully complete a yoga practice before work. This is a system for ensuring your yoga practice happens. Pick one of those habits to start implementing today and layer the other ones on as you feel ready.

Action Step: Take one of the goals that you identified in the previous chapter and break it down into its most essential steps. When I was teaching fifth grade, I would teach students how to write procedures in science class. I would ask them to write a procedure for making a peanut butter and jelly sandwich and then follow the steps exactly how the students read them to me. This was (usually) a hilarious lesson, as I was exaggeratingly slapping peanut butter on the table or putting jelly directly on top of the peanut butter. This lesson taught them that they needed to be super detailed and specific so that anyone could come in and replicate their process. You need to do the same thing as you design a system to fast-track you to your dream life.

Lastly, use a habit tracker to measure your progress and to keep you honest. The habit tracker that Darren Hardy introduced in *The Compound Effect* was a game changer for me since I am such a visual number nerd who wants to get the checkmark on the tracking sheet. Whatever will motivate you to keep up the momentum is what you want to start implementing at this stage.

Found your passions (Chapter Nine):

Several of my beta readers, when I was first introducing this book out in the world, were quick to tell me that they flipped to this chapter first. As a thirty- or forty-year-old with kids, they honestly had not had the time to think about their own passions in years. A lot of them admitted that while they knew they did not have a passion area that they were currently focused on, they wanted to make time for one soon.

"Don't make raising your childen your one and only passion."

A hard truth for parents is this: don't make raising your children your one and only passion. When I was teaching, I saw this play out over and over again. Well-meaning parents made their children the center of their whole world. Then the child would grow up and head off to college, leaving the parent completely lost on who they were, with no hobbies, passions, or interests to fill that gap. Do not be that parent. Prioritize your own interests and let your children see you do it. Who knows, maybe you will find activities that you are passionate about as a family that you can incorporate into your family life, creating memories together while your children are still at home.

Action Steps: There were so many options for different ways to explore your passion areas in Chapter Four. Go back through and choose at least one that seems vaguely interesting to you. At the very least, create a list in your MAP Book of areas that you are interested in. Notice when you are scrolling Instagram the kinds of topics that slow or stop your scroll. Add those to the list. Think about areas that you have always been interested in and never had the time to invest in. Life is happening, so take the time now to dig into those passions, even if you don't have as much bandwidth as you would like right now as a busy mom.

I am currently writing this page in the middle of busy season, when I have nine sessions this week, thirty-four mini sessions, and a full docket of editing to do, on top of room parent responsibilities, coaching clients, and a messy house to boot. How am I getting it done? I called my shot, identified my passion for writing as a priority, and am making it happen. You can do it too.

Created a three-year action plan (Chapter Ten):

Finally, here comes the heavy lifting and the culmination of all of the work on your personal growth journey that has brought you to this point. Your three-year action plan brings together your dream life vision and aligned actions that will lead you to your dream life. After determining your core values, strengthening your growth mindset, and dialing in your habits, you are ready to make your dream a reality.

Give yourself permission to dream, Mama. When I realized that I was thirty-two years old and had thirty-two years left in the classroom, I felt broken and knew I did not want to live with that feeling. I did not want to raise my children in that mental space. Even though it felt financially impossible at the time, my husband and I started to dream and turn those dreams into action. When things feel hard, ask yourself: Is this a life that I would want for my children? If the answer is a resounding no, you need to start the process of dreaming so that you can begin to evolve and grow into the person you want your kids to emulate.

Action Step: Personally, I have found the most success when I use the three-year action plan chart and backward planning method that we discussed in Chapter Ten. If this does not compute in your brain, experiment with different methods. You could journal what you want your life to look like three years from today. Then, during your next journaling session, back it up to what your life would look like two years from now, then one year from now.

If journaling isn't your style and the chart does not work for you, try a mind map at different points in time. Do not feel like your personal growth journey has to look formulaic. I promise it is worth the time to figure out what makes the most sense for your brain and what is the most motivational for you. I prefer to have my three-year action plan chart all squeezed onto a single 11x17 Google Doc page that I open once or twice a month to check in on. You may want to put it on a three-year calendar in your office or make it the background on your phone or the first page of your MAP Book.

At the end of the day, it does not matter what your action plan looks like. All that matters is that you are moving yourself, every single day, toward your dream life vision, Mama. All we have is time. Are you making the most of yours?

A
Final Word

Mama, we did it. By the time you are reading these words, you have gone through an incredible transformation, purely through absorbing the words on these pages and beginning to think bigger. Take a moment to look around you, breathe deep, and enjoy this moment. You are now armed with the information that is going to change your life, your family's life, and the generations beyond you.

That sounds dramatic to say, but I believe it is true. If you lean into your power, redesign your life, and start to live at a higher vibration than ever before, you can bet that you are changing future generations. Some day, you will be a great-great grandma who was a trailblazer, a firestarter, someone that your great-great-granddaughter will think of and say, "Man, I'm lucky to be related to her." Why? Because you are doing the scary things, breaking the mold, and truly taking advantage of the one life you have to live. Life is too short to have regrets, Mama.

This journey is never going to be easy. But remember, you are not alone. There will be challenges, there will be days when it feels easier to quit, and there will definitely be hurdles that feel insurmountable to overcome. Honestly, I truly believe that is the universe throwing you a test to see if you are for real. So put on your big girl pants and show the universe that, heck yeah, you are for real. This is where the magic happens.

What you do from here is completely up to you. Most moms go back to the beginning and get ready to make the magic happen. Others dive straight in and start the process of visualizing what life could be. Whatever path you take, know that it is the right one for you at this time. And if you need support, I am here to help you on your journey. And always, always remember this: your kids are paying attention. Start living the life you want your children to live someday. This work is so, so very important.

Keep growing. Little eyes are watching,

Sharon

Acknowledgments

As I was writing this book, I began to realize that the process was a lot like having a baby. First, there was excitement, anticipation, planning, and fun announcements. After that initial phase starts to fade, the aches and pains begin. There's the occasional "What did I do?!" meltdowns, and the anticipation of the unknown. And then, finally, after months and months of waiting, it's time to share what you created with the world. This is equal parts exhilarating, terrifying, and insanely vulnerable. Similar to the early days of parenthood, the primary feelings at this point are pure joy ... and exhaustion.

Also like when you have a baby, there are so many people to express gratitude to, who make the process run more smoothly:

First, to my husband, JoelPatrick. Thank you for inspiring me to be the best version of myself every day and for not running away when I utter the words "I have an idea!". I wouldn't be living my dream life without you by my side.

To my daughters, Aubrey and Alyssa. From the beginning, my only goal was to write this book to be able to put it in your hands. I hope you design lives that you are obsessed with and know that I will always be there to cheer you on.

This book never would have seen the light of day without the encouragement of my amazing alpha and beta readers: Carrie Goodwin, Ashley Hoebel, Amy Hoerle, Jessica Ray, Rachel Segal, and Taylor Vincenzo. Thank you so much for your kind words, encouragement, and feedback!

To my launch team, you are the reason that this book is in so many busy moms' hands and I can never thank you enough for that. My forever gratitude to Rho'Nesha Bontemps, Dawn Brys, Gia Chiarillo, Stephanie Close, Cassie Corcoran, Laura Eldridge, Christine Freiburger , Carrie Goodwin, Jessica Hacker, Amy Hoerle, Danielle Hogan, Jen Otte, Christine Patalinghug, Daniella Quartucio, Erin Rickel, Jess Ruzbasan, Rachel Segal, Casey Tanuis, Jennifer Tavello, Taylor Vincenzo, and Jill Yantz.

A huge part of the inspiration for this book came from Amanda Warfield. Thank you for your transparency, your leadership, and for leading me to a great team. Jodi Brandon, thank you for helping me to clarify my message, and huge gratitude to Laura Murray for the beautiful book design, both inside and out! And of course, a shout out to Maryssa of Pocket Editing for ensuring that this Type A former English major didn't have any typos to stress over in the final copy.

And finally, a heartfelt thank you to my coaching clients for allowing me to share your stories. You inspire this work every day and your children are lucky to have you.

Index

Action plan
Action steps, 158-162
Brainstorm, 155-157
Common struggles in
creating an, 162-169
Annual review, 110-111
Being present, 83-86
Consistent action, 66-67
Core values
Definition, 88
Importance of, 88-89
Strategically
implementing, 89-96
Dream life vision, 48-51,
55-56, 61-66, 94-96, 111-112
Goal setting
12-week goals, 114-116
Family goals, 113
Personal goals, 114
Yearly goals, 112-113
Habits
Accountability, 125-130
Habit tracking, 125-128
Positive habit exercise,
122-124
Habit tracker, 126-127
Ideal day exercise, 58-59,
76-80
Level 10 life, 46-48
Life upgrades, 172-173

MAP Book, 29-34
Mind map, 57-58
Mission statement, 91-94
Notebook system, 29-34
Overwhelm, 81-82, 118
Passions
Common struggles with
finding, 147-150
Identifying yours, 141-147
The Happiness Project,
140-141
Personal growth, 19-22
Personal growth triangle,
23-25
Quarterly check-ins,
107-108
Reflection wheel, 38-46
Systems
Benefits of, 135-137
Create your own, 132-135
Implementation, 130-132
Morning system, 133-134
"Things I Need" exercise,
75-76
Thought download, 56,
102-106
Time tracker, 72-75
Values assessment, 90-91
Vision board, 59-60
Weekly check-ins, 109

The best way to support a small business mama?

Leave
A Review!

Please take 2-3 minutes to write an honest review of your experience
with *How to Design Your Life* and post on Amazon and Goodreads to
help other busy moms get their hands on this roadmap!

About
The Author

A short five years ago, Sharon was a stressed out, mom of two, who spent her days in the classroom and her nights breathing into a paper bag. After five years of designing and working towards her dream life, Sharon is now a present mom that runs two profitable small businesses and is able to show up the way she wants every day for her husband, daughters and two yellow labs. Her goal is to teach busy moms how to create a life they are obsessed with. This is Sharon's first book.

Made in United States
North Haven, CT
11 January 2024